MORE

edibleart

DAVID PAUL LAROUSSE

MORE
edibleart

75 FRESH IDEAS
FOR GARNISHING

JOHN WILEY & SONS, INC.

New York / Chichester / Weinheim / Brisbane / Singapore / Toronto

Illustrations by Carol A. Nunnelly
Photography by Marshall Gordon

Library of Congress Cataloging-in-Publication Data:

Larousse, David Paul, 1949–
     More edible art / David Paul Larousse.
           p.   cm.
     ISBN 0-471-17639-7 (alk. paper)
       1. Garnishes (Cookery) 2. Vegetable carving. 3. Fruit carving. I. Title.
   TX740.5 L37 2000
   641.8'1—dc21   99-049568

Printed in the United States of America.

10 9 8 7 6 5 4 3 2 1

Contents

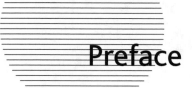

Preface

*M*ore *Edible Art* represents my personal approach and repertoire, developed through hands-on culinary experience over a period of more than two decades. The garnishes are intended to be fully utilitarian—quick and simple to prepare, and always visually engaging. The book builds on the contents of the original *Edible Art*. I will never forget, for example, the first time I watched a chef-instructor prepare a tomato rose. It was so stunning that it took what seemed to be a permanent place in my repertoire, and I doubt if I could count all the roses I have prepared since. But in spite of its beauty, I eventually came to the realization that a rolled-up strip of tomato skin does not fulfill the highest standards of gastronomic excellence. I now consider it passé, in spite of the considerable accolades it has commanded. Another rose, however, has been added, one that is fashioned from a tomato sliced paper-thin. A few garnishes have been eliminated altogether, while a number of new forms and techniques have been added. Also, a section on the basic cuts is now included, with the understanding that the cuts are an important part of and essential to high levels of culinary artistry. In all, I hope the reader finds *More Edible Art* informative and useful.

Acknowledgments

The author extends a special thanks to the following individuals: Marshall Gordon, for exceptional photography and unrivaled sense of humor; Solveig "Cookie" Hoeg of Pinelli's Flowerland, for assistance with flower terminology; Robert King of Robert King Associates, for the use of plates and platters in the photographs; David Magnusson of David Magnusson Photography, for lab backup; and Carol Nunnelly, for her gorgeous illustrations.

Introduction

My interest in garnishing began in a garde-manger class during a two-year culinary training more than two decades ago. Apple birds were among the students' most popular creations, as were tomato roses, fluted mushrooms, and roses carved from yellow and white turnips. The realism genre embraced items more whimsical than functional: a palm tree—half a green bell pepper with a zigzag edge inverted over a carrot held vertical by a toothpick; a mouse—a hard-boiled egg decorated with two radish-slice ears, a pair of clove eyes, and six 1-inch pieces of uncooked spaghetti whiskers; and a duck— a carrot bill stuck in the thin end of a yellow crookneck squash, with two cloves for eyes. None of these latter creations were ever seen or used beyond our years at school, but the faux creatures and tropical foliage were part of the experience and, along with the more functional mock flowers, they served to spark in us a genuine interest in fruit and vegetable sculpture. And for those of us who found this work engaging and challenging, over the ensuing years we continued to develop our repertoires and our styles—both the actual sculpted pieces as well as the appropriate use of that repertoire in culinary production.

In truth, it hasn't been very long since the spiced apple–lemon wedge–parsley sprig–orange slice school of garnishing ruled. This mid-twentieth-century plateau was raised to the next level, painfully and slowly, by the growth and expansion of culinary training schools as well as the dining public's collective evolution toward a heightened appreciation of culinary excellence. How many times was I admonished to attend to the eye appeal of a plate or dish during my training? Certainly more times than the number of kitchen classrooms I encountered, yet little information was conferred as to the origin of that phrase. Many years later I was fortunate to come across a history of the Paris Ritz, and in it I stumbled across what I believe to be the origin of the concept of eye appeal.

This tale began in 1867, with seventeen-year-old César Ritz coming off two discouraging experiences as an apprentice wine waiter. Unwilling to return home in disgrace, he relocated from his native Switzerland to Paris and secured work as a waiter—first at a workmen's bistro, then at a luncheon restaurant—from which he was fired for breaking too many dishes. At a third eatery, he worked his way up from assistant waiter to manager (and had an affair with a Russian baroness in the process). At this point, Ritz was informed enough to know where the important restaurant action was, so much so that when he was offered a partnership in this third eatery, he declined, choosing instead to seek employment at a more fashionable establishment. That establishment was Restaurant Voisin, and young Ritz presented himself to the maître d'. Monsieur Bellenger was initially unimpressed with Ritz, in spite of his fluency in four languages and his further claims of being "quick, neat, polite, and experienced in all aspects of restaurant work." Sensing Bellenger's lukewarm response, Ritz lowered his guard and said, "I am willing to start at the beginning and learn if you will teach me." Impressed with this sudden display of humility, Bellenger engaged him on the spot as an assistant waiter and, over the years there, Ritz became well known among the clientele, which included Sarah Bernhardt, Edmond de Goncourt, George Sand, and Alexandre Dumas (*fils*). But the key incident of which I write had to do with the maître d's task of carving roasts at tableside. Bellenger trained the young Ritz to take on that job; his instructions included the specific technique of pressing the fork into the roast, which compelled the internal juices to run out. This, according to Bellenger, was of major significance, as it gave what he termed an "appeal to the eye."

This lesson was not wasted on the man who, as a wine apprentice, was once told, "You will never make anything of yourself in the hotel business. It requires a special flair and . . . you don't have it." Indeed, César Ritz went on to become quite possibly the most influential hotelier in the Western world. Hence, anything that transpired within his sphere had the potential to find its way into the culinary trade either during his life or for a considerable time after. And it was this experience with Bellenger, this shared little trick of the trade intended to enhance the appearance of a dish, this "appeal to the eye," that evolved into one of the most oft-repeated admonitions in culinary training programs more than a century later. Furthermore, the concept became an essential foundation from which we students developed our garnishing repertoires—both the simple and the advanced additions to a plate or platter.

The Origin of *Edible Art*

After a decade of working in the profession and developing my repertoire, I arrived at a juncture where the art in the "culinary arts" and my own creativity came together. Yet as an artist working in a food medium, this was not cause for celebration. There was an element of frustration—for the art was forever disappearing. This was a quandary that I was unprepared for, and it required serious contemplation. Ultimately, the solution was to combine the two—art and food—and put it into permanent form. The result of that effort was *Edible Art*, a how-to text on the art of garnishing. The contents of this book, this "art that you eat," also had a subtext in the form of a term that evolved in classes in which I taught the genre. That term was *California mukimono—Mukimono* is a Japanese word meaning "to slice things"; California is both my birthplace and the locale where I cut important teeth in the development of my culinary repertoire. And assigning a name to this whole genre of food sculpture gave it an air of official authenticity that elevated it above and beyond the parsley sprig–orange slice–spiced apple–lemon wedge school.

Two fundamental characteristics form the hallmark of California mukimono: it is (1) visually stunning, as in gorgeous, and (2) highly functional, as in relatively quick and easy to prepare. This is not to say that garnishing cannot be complex or sculptural, but California mukimono is unique in its simplicity and functionality. These characteristics come from an awareness of the time restraints and labor demands in most kitchens, and I have thus always endeavored to develop items that are time effective and simple to prepare. A lavish party or formal competition may warrant extra time and attention, but these garnishing techniques are predicated on an acute awareness of the usual importance of economy of time and motion.

At this point, it is important to acknowledge other practitioners, whose work is nothing less than astounding and rivals classical sculpture in any culture. I have seen all manner of mangos, melons, papaya, squash, and oversized root vegetables carved into the most intricate forms, imitating lanterns and bridges, dragons and birds, ocean creatures and royal dogs, mythical heroes and wild beasts. This kind of work, for me, has always been inspiring, but it is not within my own personal realm of creation. My style is firmly rooted in efficient beauty—visually pleasing work that can be prepared well within the time frame of the production hours available for a given event or events. For California mukimono to exist, this line must be adhered to.

Additionally, the practitioner should know that, as in any creative medium, there is no end to the potential for variation; California mukimono is truly a limitless realm. When mukimono artists carve together, the synergy often moves styles and garnishes in unexpected ways. An eight-petal flower motif, which I had learned years before from an Asian instructor, traditionally was applied to an apple. In a more recent practice session with a colleague, I watched as he applied the same cut to a small square of daikon radish, and it took on an entirely different character (see Daikon Celestial Cube, page 66). I have seen students come up with unexpected innovations as well. I recall one who cut no fewer than thirteen wedges in the process of creating an apple feather—a piece that I was accustomed to cutting to a maximum of eight wedges. In conclusion, it is important for the reader to remember that for every flower form or garnish revealed in this book, there is ample room for mukimono artists to take it to another level or to add a unique dimension that will make the piece their own. Indeed, creative license is not only encouraged, it is encouraged and embraced.

A Word About Socles

*S*ocle (pronounced *sock-ul*) is an architectural term defined as "a plain square block higher than a plinth, serving as a pedestal for sculpture, a vase, or a column." I do not know who first borrowed this word and applied it in a culinary context (although *socle* is easier on the ear than *plinth*). However, in this new use, socle has come to refer to any form of food container fashioned from food. This, then, includes quite a broad range of traditional as well as contemporary innovations.

A *croustade* is one of the most basic and traditional forms of socle; it is made from any of a number of farinaceous foods (rich in starch). Typically a croustade consists of a thick slice of bread or a small roll hollowed out, brushed with butter, baked until brown and crisp, then filled with some variety of mousse, salad, salpicon, stew, vegetable, or purée.

Croustades may also be fashioned from puff pastry (for bouchées), pâte à choux (for carolines and duchesses, also known as éclairs and puffs), short dough (for barquettes and tartlets), phyllo, duchesse potatoes, pasta, polenta, or rice. They are baked, usually in a mold, removed from the mold, then filled as desired.

Tomatoes also have a long tradition of service as containers. Examples include Tomatoes Bonne Femme (sausage, onion, bread, garlic, parsley), Clamart (puréed green peas), Monasqué (Russian salad topped with a piece of tuna), Parisienne (sausage, truffle, mushrooms), and Piémontais (tomato risotto).

Other vegetable socles include bell peppers, cabbage (whole or leaves), eggplant, grape leaves (for Greek dolmas), onions, potatoes, and zucchini. Fruits are also used in this fashion, typically avocado, melon, orange, pear, and apple. In modern times, other vegetables are seen carved into miniature socles; these include jícama, daikon, red radish, yellow crookneck squash, cherry tomatoes, and zucchini. Tortilla triangles are brushed with oil, as are wonton skins (which are then pressed into small muffin tins), then baked and used as hors d'oeuvre bases.

Finally, a number of vegetables can be cut into small circular and cylindrical forms that are used as miniature collars (see Lattice Squash Collar, page 113, and color photo of collars). These include carrot, cucumber, bell pepper, yellow squash, and zucchini.

The Application of Garnishes

Garnishing can be divided up into two categories: integral and nonintegral. Integral garnishes are part of a specific dish: the julienned parsley-flavored crêpe in Consommé Celestine; the miniature cucumber ovals for Sole Doria; the vegetable brunoise (very fine dice) in the whiskey-flavored cream sauce that accompanies Breast of Chicken Catherine de Medici; the tournéed vegetables for Roast Lamb Rack Bouquetière; the diced fruit in a Diplomat Pudding; and so on. Nonintegral garnishes consist of fruits and vegetables that have been sculpted, sliced, or otherwise shaped into flower or geometric forms, then used to embellish individual dishes or buffet presentations. These are generally not bound by any traditional guidelines, though there may be an occasional exception. Consider Beijing (formerly Peking) Duck, consisting of pieces of crispy skin, sliced duck meat, hoisin sauce, a double scallion brush, and a simple crêpe to wrap them all in—the scallion flower is simply the traditional garnish for the dish.

For the most part, nonintegral garnishes are used as an adjunct to highlight a dish or large platter presentation. Their use is determined by the individual responsible for preparing that dish, though there are important considerations behind such use. Simplicity, economy, and discretion are important, even if solely from the standpoint of time and labor. To borrow a phrase from M.F.K. Fisher, the use of garnishes should be "like birds in a tree—where there is a comfortable branch."

It is also recommended that a garnish be applied to a dish as an indicator of an ingredient within—in other words, something with a connection to the dish. An imprinted mushroom poached in white wine, then set atop a mushroom omelet, makes perfect sense, as does a radish rose for Grilled Squab accompanied by a radish salsa (Juan Paiz's Salsa: radish, scallion cilantro, jalapeño, lime juice); scallion flowers on a dish of roasted red onions glazed with balsamic vinegar; a Carrot Zinnia for Potage Crécy (a puréed carrot soup); cucumber loops on a piece of grilled fish Doria (a cucumber-garnished sauce); an apple feather with a cheese course; and so on.

Finally, there is another interesting facet of philosophy behind the importance of garnishing and of the whole visual experience involved with dining. The late

Henri Charpentier (1880–1961), inventor of Crêpes Suzette,[1] held the sandwich, an English invention, in horror, because it effectively hides the food one is about to ingest. In his 1934 autobiography, *Life à la Henri* (Simon & Schuster), Charpentier recorded the counsel of his mentor, Jean Camous: "A man should always see what he eats [because] . . . the eyes and the nose give the signals for the release of the chemical fluids which are secreted in the body by an intelligence of tremendous significance in the philosophy of a chef—the intelligence of the inner man." This takes the concept of eye appeal to a deeper level and fortifies another dictum revealed to students during culinary training—that we eat with our eyes first.

[1]Working as a *commis du rang* (assistant waiter) at the Café de Paris in Monte Carlo in 1895, young Henri was given an opportunity to prepare a dessert for a party hosted by Edward, Prince of Wales, who was accompanied by seven other gentlemen, one of whom had brought his daughter. He created a dish, similar to one he had often tasted as a young boy, that consisted of crêpes drenched with a sauce prepared from butter and three liquors: maraschino, Curaçao, and Kirschwasser. Henri wrote the following account: "The Prince asked me the name of that which he had eaten with so much relish. I told him it was to be called Crêpes Princesse. He recognized it as a compliment to the young lady present. She was alert and rose to her feet and holding her little skirt wide with her hands she made him a curtsey. The Prince responded: 'Will you change the name from Crêpes Princesse to Crêpes Suzette?' And so this confection was born and named, one taste of which, I really believe, would reform a cannibal into a civilized gentleman."

Understanding the Cutting Blade

Prince Huei's cook was cutting with his knife, and every *chhk* of the chopper was in perfect rhythm. "Well done!" cried the prince. "Yours is skill indeed!"

"Sire," replied the cook, laying down his blade, "I have always devoted myself to Tao [pronounced "dow"], which is higher than mere skill. When I first began to cut up different food items, I saw the whole item, but after three years' practice I no longer viewed them in this way. I work with my mind and not with my eye or through control of the senses. I glide through great joints or delicate vegetables according to the natural constitution of the thing being cut.

"A good cook rarely changes his blade, because he cuts. An ordinary cook must change his blade once a month, because he hacks. I have had this knife for nineteen years, and although I have cut up a thousand bulls and ten thousand cabbages, its edge is as if fresh from the whetstone." (Adapted by the author from *The Butcher's Knife* by Chuangtse [335–275 B.C.], from *The Book of Chuangtse*, as seen in *The Importance of Understanding: Translations from the Chinese* by Lin Yutang, © 1960, World Publishing)

Some years ago I worked in a large multirestaurant operation with a central kitchen where all the basic preparations for five different restaurant operations were produced. David Yung was the butcher who filleted, trimmed, and boned hundreds of pounds of beef, veal, pork, poultry, and fish each week. Several times a year I would gather the other cooks' knives and drop them at a cutlery shop that skillfully renewed the cutting edges on the tools. I always asked David if he had any knives he wanted tuned up, and he always declined. The only sharpening device he used was a very old, well-worn steel, which he used periodically throughout the day in a rather frantic manner as he tore through his workload. Chuangtse's parable on cutlery may be a bit corny, but after witnessing the principle in action, it is not easily explained by Western methodology. For it is not the tools that make the craftsman but the ability of the craftsman who is using those tools. To this day, I marvel at my memory of the butcher whose work symbolized an ancient Taoist principle—working in harmony with the food items he was cutting. He was able to break down great quantities of raw food materials in a way that never depleted the edge on his tools.

Cutlery handling is a personal learning experience that requires time spent with one's tools in order to understand their physicality and how to maintain a sharp edge. A sharpening stone of some kind is essential, though one should avoid electric sharpeners. If not properly used, these gadgets can excessively grind down an expensive precision-made knife, designed to last several decades, in a few short years. The carborundum tri-stones that sit in a well containing mineral oil are effective, but they are expensive and heavy, and they invariably become coated with mineral oil. I have found my best success with a ceramic tri-stone, manufactured by a 150-year-old New England company, that is efficient and lightweight, requires no lubrication, and is easily disassembled. (See Appendix for information on the Dexter Three-Way Sharpening Stone.)

As for technique, that will vary as well. Most culinarians, when applying a knife to a sharpening stone, move the knife across the stone into the cutting edge of the knife. Others (including me) move the knife away from the cutting edge. Whichever method is used, it should be applied in the same direction on both sides of the blade and should be done evenly—each stroke matched on its opposite side.

The angle at which the knife is held should be fairly low, around 15 degrees. The motion of the knife should run the full length of the surface of the stone (so the stone will not wear unevenly over time); that motion should be firm and smooth. The number of swipes depends on how dull the knife is but, generally, ten to fifteen suffice. To determine if the knife has been sufficiently sharpened on a stone, stroke the knife on a steel, then cut a small piece of food.

Occasionally, no matter how careful one is with tools, a knife may become gouged, a tip may snap off, or the convex form of the cutting blade may become so worn that it grows concave. In such a case, the knife requires regrinding to restore its proper shape. Most major urban areas have at least one establishment that specializes in the sale and restoration of cutlery. It is important, however, to be aware that not everyone who performs such work does so in the same professional manner. I recall a knife I brought to a shop many years ago that, when returned, had lost about a quarter of its size, and even then wasn't particularly sharp. So, let the buyer beware—be very clear about the process used to reshape your cutlery and interview the person who will execute it.

Philosophies of Cutlery

In discussing individual philosophies behind the use of kitchen cutlery and tools, we begin with the two broadest extremes—minimalists on one end, maximalists on the other. The minimalists are those who can accomplish virtually all cutting tasks with a single tool—typically, a traditional Chinese cleaver. On the other end of the spectrum are the maximalists, whose primary tool is the French, or cook's knife but who also use innumerable other tools for scores of different functions. In practice, nearly everyone lies somewhere in between.

The differences between the Chinese cleaver and the French knife are fascinating. The Chinese cleaver, for example, reveals a certain ancient wisdom in three specific ways. First, because of its relatively large, broad blade, it doubles as a carrying device—after ingredients are cut, they are transported on the flat surface of the blade to a holding area before cooking commences. Second, that same broad plane can be used to crush garlic, ginger, and other spices, in one fell swoop. And third, the front edge of the knife is vertical as opposed to pointed, indicating that it was designed to be a cutting tool from its inception, and not a weapon first and cutting device second. Thus it is, by its very design, a highly functional and utilitarian utensil.

A French knife, on the other hand, evolved from a fighting implement carried in a scabbard at the waist. When not engaged in fighting, the warrior would use the blade to cut and eat food. Thus, its original primary function had little to do with creating fine victuals.

In recent years, however, some innovations in design have brought about important changes to the cleaver school. First, many Western manufacturers have been producing a Chinese-style cleaver for some time. Second, more recently, manufacturers, both in Europe and the United States, have taken the forms of the two knives—the French knife and the cleaver—and combined them. This has resulted in knives fabricated from the highest quality steel, combined with a surface area that is slightly broader than that of a French knife and a rounded instead of a pointed front edge. Lastly, some media-celebrated chefs have begun to offer signature cleavers that are manufactured using the same high-quality steel used in the Western knives. This has been a boon to Western practitioners who have explored the use of cleavers and have found how efficient they can be for certain tasks.

Today, there are so many manufacturers offering so many different types of knives in such a broad range of styles and prices, that it is sometimes difficult to make a wise purchasing decision. Nevertheless, as the market interest in cutlery continues unabated, manufacturers continue to try to meet that demand. One specific example of this has been the innovation of a new generation of knives, developed in Japan—knives that are unique in both design and blade material. In 1985, Konin Yamada, a tool designer, was given a full range of unlimited resources to design a kitchen knife that would be comfortable, easy to handle, and yet meet the rigorous requirements of the most demanding professionals. The result was a knife developed in the same tradition as the handcrafted swords created for the Samauri, Japan's ancient warrior caste. Yoshikin is the company that manufactures these tools, under the brand name Global, and its claim that it has reinvented professional cutlery is not far from the truth. Its knives are handcrafted from a molybdenum/vanadium alloy that permits the creation of a cutting edge that keeps its razor-sharp edge longer than any other steel. These tools are also extraordinarily thin and well balanced, and their unique, seamless construction not only eliminates food and dirt traps but also makes them exceptionally easy to use. Today, there are more than seventy different types of Global knives and kitchen utensils.

Specialty Tools

In spite of the theory of minimalism, some cutting maneuvers simply cannot be performed with the cleaver. For particularly fine work, both a paring knife and a bird's-beak paring knife are indispensable. Also, spherical cuts are essential in certain instances. Such cuts require a Parisienne scoop—a device equipped with a large and a medium sphere (Parisienne and noisette, respectively), as well as the smaller single pois scoops (*pois* means "pea") that allow the chef to make smaller spheres. These spheres are fashioned from various vegetables and used as garnishes in salads, soups, small dishes, main courses, and desserts. (It is a cut I am particularly fond of, and these tools are an essential part of my kit.)

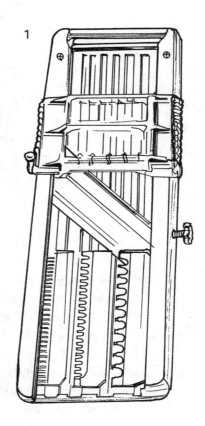

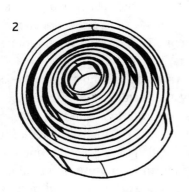

1. Japanese mandoline with guard and three blades— fine, medium, large
2. Set of round cutters

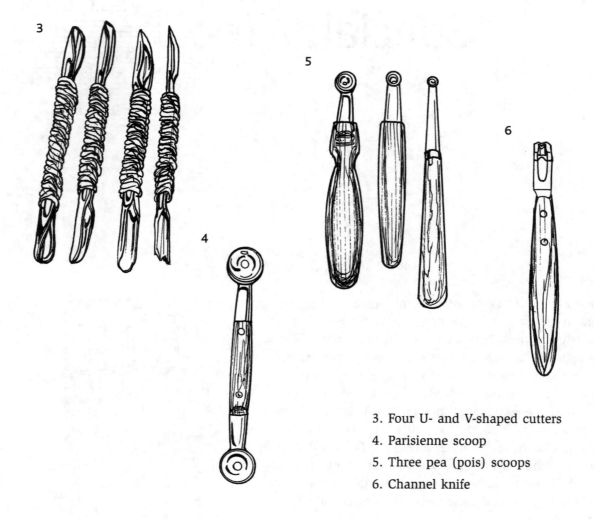

3. Four U- and V-shaped cutters
4. Parisienne scoop
5. Three pea (pois) scoops
6. Channel knife

Another family of inexpensive yet highly functional tools consists of a variety of different sized *V*- and *U*-shaped cutters. These are made from a sheet of stamped metal, then rolled into uncomplicated and basic tools. They work best on root vegetables and succulent fruits—melon, apples, pears, papaya.

Finally, a four-piece set of vegetable cutters (available at most Asian houseware and cutlery suppliers, or through specialty tool catalogs; see Appendix of Specialty Suppliers) consists of round cutters that are used to create four different flowers; the set is available in two diameters: 1 inch and 1½ inches. Three of the four flower forms are five-petaled, including one with pointed petals, one with rounded petals, and one with notched petals. The fourth form presents a scalloped edge with a dozen round mini-petals. These cutters are extremely useful in mukimono work.

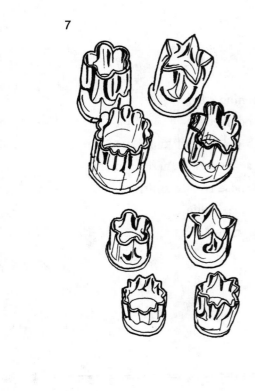

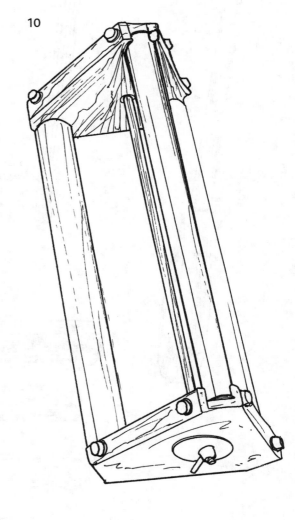

7. Two different-sized sets of floral cutters (4 + 4)
8. Small portable steel
9. Small carborundum stone
10. Three-way knife sharpener (Russell-Dexter)

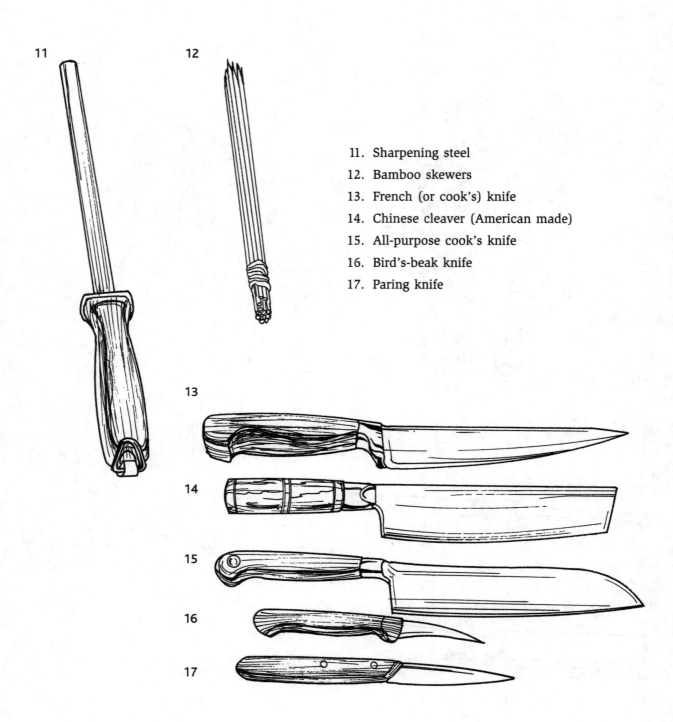

11. Sharpening steel
12. Bamboo skewers
13. French (or cook's) knife
14. Chinese cleaver (American made)
15. All-purpose cook's knife
16. Bird's-beak knife
17. Paring knife

Suggestions on How to Use Mukimono

Some years ago, I set a small watermelon on a specially constructed platform and covered it with mukimono flowers held on toothpicks. It was intended to be an entry in a formal food competition in New York City. Initially, my compatriots thought it far too modern and artsy for a competition within the classic buffet category, but it was nevertheless transported along with thirty other entries. The primary centerpiece for the table was a large deer fashioned from salt dough and, as fate would have it, the deer was damaged in transit beyond repair. My mukimono bouquet suddenly became an essential part of our table.

There are no specific rules regarding the use of the garnishes shown in this text—it is very much a matter of personal taste and style. Keeping M.F.K. Fisher's admonition in mind, it is wise to offer decorative visual points for your guests in a judicious manner—just enough to pique their interest, but not so much that they are distracted from the experience of the entire meal. Garnishes also work well on large offerings of food, such as the holiday roast turkey platter or a charcuterie layout (cold, sliced meat, fish, and poultry). Small arrangements of baby vegetables and sculpted flowers can be attractive when placed on a whole Brie or large block of cheese. Beyond this, each mukimono artist develops a personal style and method of placement.

Special Preparation Notes

- I encourage you to be patient in the process of learning the techniques revealed herein. Just as with any skill, much practice is required to reach a level of competent ability.

- Remember that your mukimono garnishes and centerpieces are edible, meaning that your guests may eat your artful creations. To prepare for such eventualities—it is a compliment—be careful to remove hidden toothpicks. If a garnish requires that a toothpick be left in place to hold it together, make sure the toothpick remains in clear view.

- In the process of creating mukimono flowers and flower forms, it is important to find secondary uses for trim. Carrot, celery, and onion pieces can be utilized in stocks; the trim from other vegetables—bell pepper, leek, scallion, turnip, zucchini, and so on—can often be utilized in soups, both broth-based and puréed. There will, however, always be some parts of vegetables and fruits that have little secondary use. This includes all vegetable peelings as well as items such as radish leaves, orange peel, small scraps of daikon, and so on. They do have tremendous value, however, when returned to the soil in the form of compost. The Culinary Institute of America in Hyde Park, New York, has made composting on a large scale politically correct. I was a student there in 1973, when folk music legend Pete Seeger came to speak. His topic was recycling, and his message included a song—which I will never forget—entitled "Garbage Is Gold." I'm pleased to report that The Culinary Institute took Mr. Seeger's suggestion—even if it took them twenty years to get there—and their kitchens now cart all food scraps out to the farms in the Hudson River Valley area. They also purchase the nutritionally revitalized soil that results from composting and use it on their grounds.

- All fruits and vegetables should be rinsed in cold water before using.

- All vegetables that are typically peeled should be peeled before carving. These include carrots, daikon, white and yellow onions, and turnips.

- Certain varieties of *apple* tend to bruise more than others, so be careful which you select. (I prefer Granny Smith apples.)

- One variety of very fat carrots, whose agricultural name is "Danvers Half-long" and that are sometimes referred to as "horse carrots," tend to have a woody center, but they are excellent for carving purposes. They are also difficult to come by, so I recommend requesting the fattest carrots possible from your local produce supplier; suppliers are usually willing to cull the broader varieties as long as you provide advance notice.

- Perhaps Samuel Johnson (1709–1784) was fed too many cucumbers as a child. He wrote, "A cucumber should be well-sliced, dressed with pepper and vinegar, and then thrown out." They are, however, an excellent sculpting medium, and hothouse cucumbers are the recommended variety for sculpting for several reasons: they contain fewer seeds than the supermarket variety; they possess a thin, tender skin that is easily cut into; and they are not coated with fat, oil, or any other substance.

- During production—and later, when a flower or form is set out—an occasional spritz from a small plastic spray bottle filled with cold water helps prevent fruits and vegetables from drying out.

- The measurements provided for where or how far to make a cut are intended only as guidelines. For example, if the guidelines suggest making an incision "down to approximately ¼ inch (6 mm) from the bottom" and the incision can be made a little closer to the bottom, permitting a flower to open up a little more, so much the better.

- Methods of storing mukimono flowers until ready to use vary. Common sense is a good guide, and preferences vary as well. A list of suggested storage methods follows.

GARNISHES BEST STORED ON A PLATE OR DISH COVERED WITH A DAMP TOWEL OR PLASTIC WRAP AND REFRIGERATED FOR UP TO A HALF DAY

Beet Pinwheels

Spiked Beet Stems

Cucumber Fan and Loops

Cucumber Lilies

Leek Braids

Leek and Scallion Ties

Mushroom Imprints

Radish Feathers

Tomato Roses

Zucchini Asters

All fruit flowers and forms

GARNISHES BEST STORED IN ICE WATER FOR UP TO A HALF DAY

Acorn Squash Flowers

Bell Pepper Baskets

Cucumber flowers and forms

Onion Chrysanthemums

Onion Artichokes

Onion Magnolias (Begonias)

Zucchini Crowns

Zucchini Five-Petal Flowers

GARNISHES THAT CAN BE STORED FOR EXTENDED PERIODS IMMERSED IN ICE WATER[1]

All carrot flowers and forms

All celery flowers

All jalapeño flowers

Leek and scallion leaves and brushes

All daikon radish and red radish flowers and forms

All turnip flowers and forms (purple-top white turnips and rutabagas)

[1]The water should be changed every 48 hours.

The Basic Cuts

The attention the culinary practitioner pays to the cutting of garnishes is critical. Cutting is the key area where a culinarian transforms raw food materials into various shapes and forms, demonstrating passion for the craft and commitment to details. When a dining patron lifts a spoonful of soup or forkful of vegetables, the precision (or otherwise) with which those vegetable garnishes have been cut becomes starkly clear. It is at this moment that the skill of the cook is laid bare. For this reason, it is of the utmost importance that garnishes be cut consistently and uniformly. This moment is an opportunity to demonstrate the care taken to transform nature's ordinary ingredients into a visually splendid and carefully executed gastronomic effort.

Here is a list of the cuts used in the culinary craft. It is intended as a guide, as nomenclature and dimensions vary considerably among kitchens and practitioners.

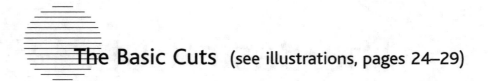

The Basic Cuts (see illustrations, pages 24–29)

Potatoes   Les Pommes de Terre

English	*French*	*Description*
straw	paille	a thin ribbon[1]
chip	chip	a thin uniform slice
waffle	gaufrette	a crisscrossed slice
matchstick	allumette	$1/8 \times 1/8 \times 1\frac{1}{2}$ inches
French fries	frite	$1/4 \times 1/4 \times 2\text{–}2\frac{1}{2}$ inches
steak fries	pont-neuf	$1/2 \times 1/2 \times 3$ inches
medium dice	parmentier	$1/3\text{–}1/2$-inch cube
large dice	carré	$1/2\text{–}3/4$-inch cube
noisette	noisette	a small ball or sphere
parisienne	parisienne	a large ball or sphere
turned	tourné	7-sided oval
small	château	$1\frac{1}{2}$ inches long
medium	nature	$2\text{–}2\frac{1}{2}$ inches long
large	fondante	$2\frac{1}{2}\text{–}3$ inches long

[1]While straw potatoes are generally cut on the serrated cutting edge of a stainless-steel mandoline, they can also be cut on a plastic mandoline using the very fine blade. (See Figure 1.) Other vegetables, such as carrot, cucumber, daikon, yellow squash, and zucchini, can be cut using the medium blade, creating a vegetable "spaghetti." Blanched, drained, then blended with a hot or cold sauce (such as a cream sauce, velouté, or vinaigrette), they make excellent side dishes.

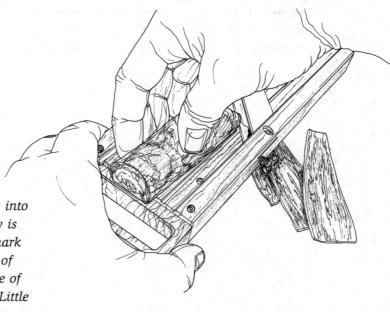

Figure 1 *When cutting the vegetables into julienned and diced forms, uniformity is not only essential, it is also the hallmark of professionalism and an expression of passion for the work at hand. The use of a mandoline—such as the Japanese "Little Beni" mandoline shown here—is an important aid in achieving that uniformity.*

Vegetables | Les Legumes

English	French	Description
small dice	brunoise	⅛-inch cube (see Figure 2)
medium dice	jardinière[2]	¼-inch cube (see Figure 3)
large dice	macedoine[3]	⅓–½-inch cube (see Figure 3)
julienne	julienne[4]	⅛ × ⅛ × 1 inch (see Figure 4)
large julienne	batonnet	¼ × ¼ × 2–2½ inches (see Figure 5)
diamond	losange	size varies according to use[5] (see Figure 6; for a variation, see Figures 7 and 8)
pea (also *pearl*)	pois (*perle*)	a tiny ball or sphere (see Figure 9)
medium sphere	noisette	a medium ball or sphere (see Figure 9)
parisienne	parisienne	a large ball or sphere (see Figures 9, 10, and 11)
rough cut	paysanne	a rough, unequal cut
thin sliced	Vichy	a thin circular slice
turned	tourné	7-sided oval, 1–1½ inches long (see Figures 12 and 13)
slivered (also *shredded*)	chiffonade	a thin ribbon, usually for green leafy vegetables

[2]Jardinière means "of the garden," a loose reference to the origin of vegetables.

[3]Macedoine has its origins in ancient Macedonia, the area comprising modern-day Iran, Greece, and Egypt, ruled over by Alexander the Great (356–323 B.C.) from 336 to 323 B.C.; common usage: medley or mixture.

[4]Vichy is a town in central France whose natural hot springs make it a celebrated spa. The use of the term here is a bit of a stretch, derived from a dish typical of the region—Vichy Carrots—which are thin-sliced carrots simmered in mineral water and seasoned with chopped parsley (no fat, no salt).

[5]Technically known as a *rhombus*—a four-sided figure formed by two inner obtuse and two inner acute angles.

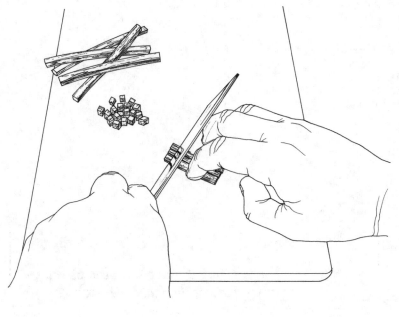

Figure 2 *The julienne strips can be cut into a fine dice (brunoise).*

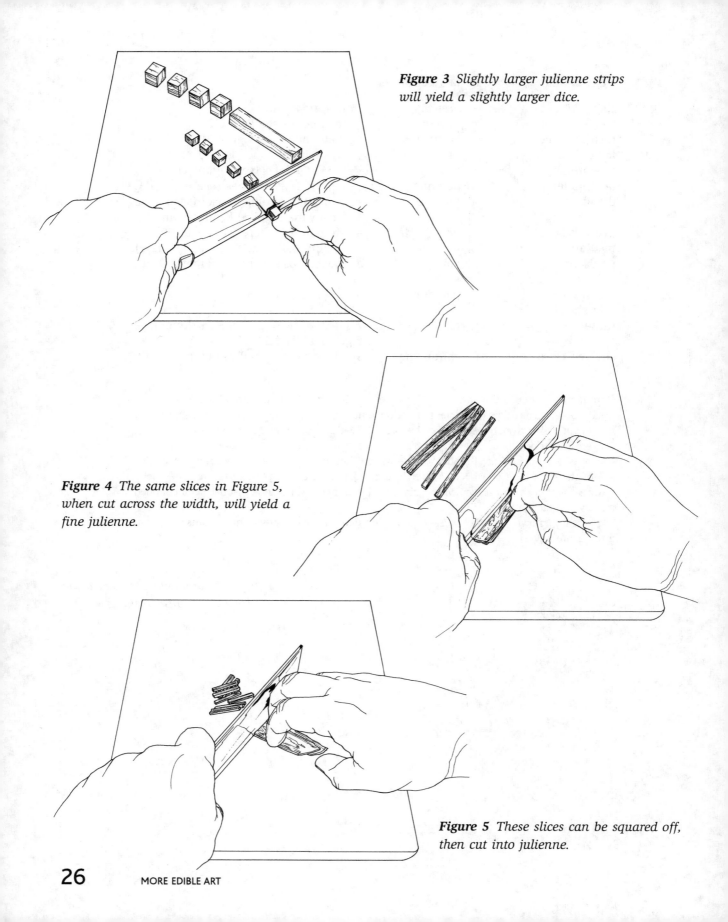

Figure 3 *Slightly larger julienne strips will yield a slightly larger dice.*

Figure 4 *The same slices in Figure 5, when cut across the width, will yield a fine julienne.*

Figure 5 *These slices can be squared off, then cut into julienne.*

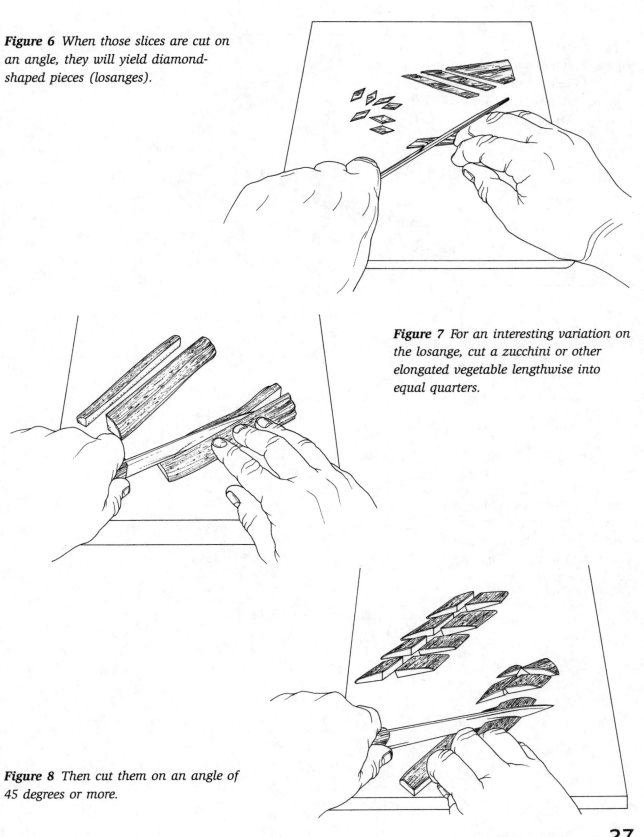

Figure 6 *When those slices are cut on an angle, they will yield diamond-shaped pieces (losanges).*

Figure 7 *For an interesting variation on the losange, cut a zucchini or other elongated vegetable lengthwise into equal quarters.*

Figure 8 *Then cut them on an angle of 45 degrees or more.*

Figure 9 In addition to the two-sided parisienne scoop, there are a number of pea (pois) scoops, two of which are shown here.

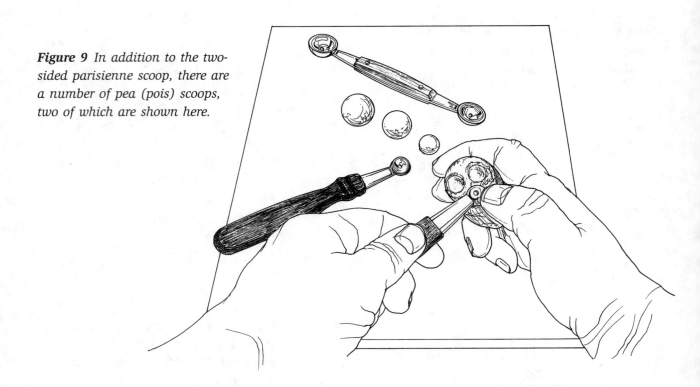

Figure 10 When cutting a large sphere (parisienne), it is a good idea to press on the cutter with your thumb while working the tool back and forth into the vegetable.

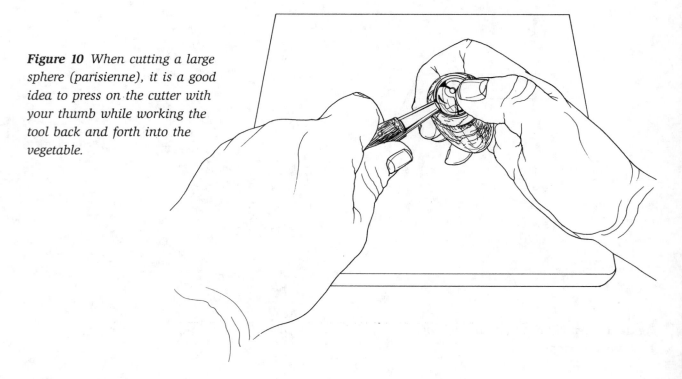

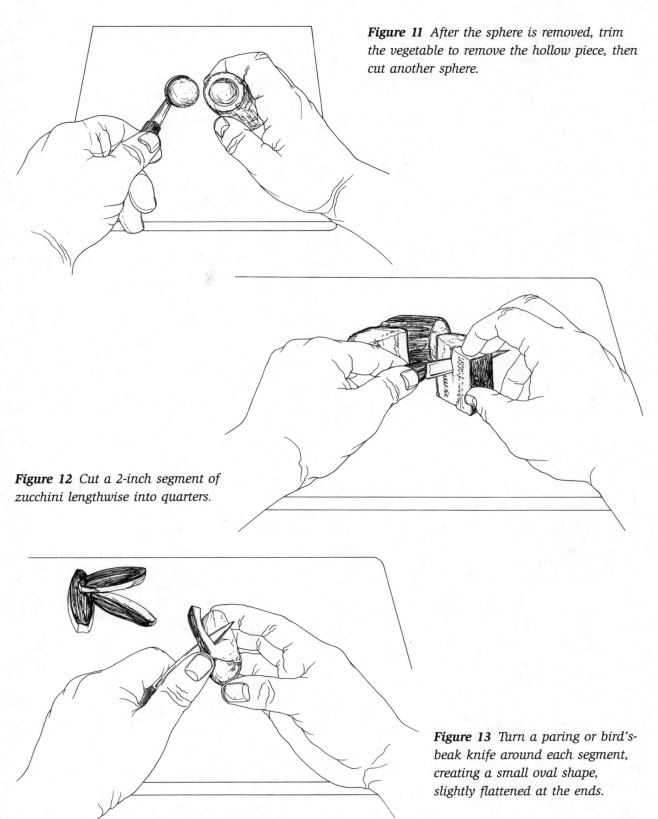

Figure 11 *After the sphere is removed, trim the vegetable to remove the hollow piece, then cut another sphere.*

Figure 12 *Cut a 2-inch segment of zucchini lengthwise into quarters.*

Figure 13 *Turn a paring or bird's-beak knife around each segment, creating a small oval shape, slightly flattened at the ends.*

Vegetable Garnishes

Ideally, a garnish that is applied to a dish functions as an indicator of, or an extension of, an ingredient within the dish. For example, you might see an imprinted mushroom poached in white wine and set atop a mushroom omelet; a radish rose for Grilled Squab accompanied by a radish salsa; a Carrot Zinnia for Potage Crécy (a puréed carrot soup); cucumber loops on a piece of grilled fish Doria (which uses a cucumber-garnished sauce).

But this rule is not cast in stone. Adding an arrangement of baby vegetables and sculpted flowers to a plate of cheeses works because they harmonize gastronomically with one's palette. The same applies to crisp, sculpted vegetables, such as radishes and scallions, set upon a holiday platter of roasted meat or poultry, or daikon daisies and rutabaga roses in the center of an arrangement of sliced Gravlax (dry-cured salmon).

But in whatever way you decide to use your garnishes, it is important to use them with restraint. They should offer decorative visual points for your guests—just enough to pique their interest, but not so much that they are distracted from the experience of the entire meal.

Acorn Squash

ACORN SQUASH RANUNCULA

Cut the squash in half lengthwise and scoop out the seeds. Cut one of the halves in half widthwise, then, using an electric slicer or mandoline, shave paper-thin slices of squash from the initial cut surface. Roll one of the slices, then wrap that with a second slice, and a third, and so on, until a flower of an appropriate size is created. Secure with one or two toothpicks and place in ice water. *Note:* Because the squash is curved, each slice is also curved. Be sure to apply each slice so that the curve is facing the same direction.

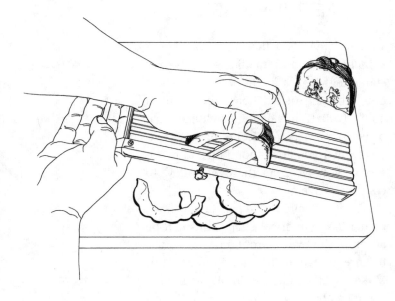

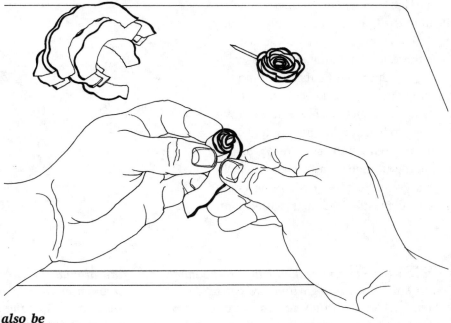

TIP *A ranuncula can also be fashioned from finely sliced apple.*

Beet

BEET PINWHEEL

Select large beets that measure at least 3 inches (75 mm) in diameter. Cut off stalks and leaves at the top of the beet and set them aside. Roast the beets at 400°F (200°C) in a pan filled with an inch of water for 1½ to 2 hours or until tender enough to allow a toothpick to be inserted. Remove from the oven, allow to cool, then peel.

Trim the circumference of the beet, giving it a cylindrical shape (this can be accomplished with a round pastry cutter; be sure to save the trim for another dish). Make a vertical incision in the side of the cylinder, about ¼ to ⅜ inch (6 to 10 mm) deep, pointed toward the center. Make a second incision about ¼ inch (6 mm) ahead of the first cut and slightly off center so that a small strip of beet falls away (save these strips for another use as well).

Repeat this pair of cuts all around the circumference of the beet, then cut the beet into thin slices using a sharp knife or a mandoline. Set the slices onto a dish, cover, and refrigerate until ready to use as a border design or as a component in a salad. *Note:* Be careful where beets are placed—they will bleed their scarlet color.

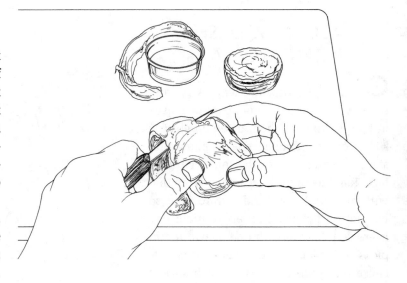

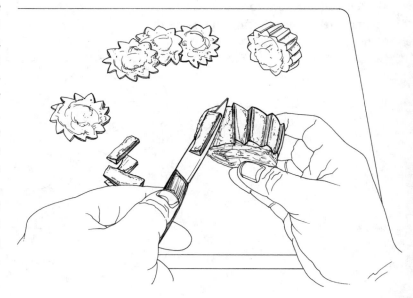

TIP *Carrots and daikon can also be made into pinwheels, though they are cut while in their raw state. Simply take a piece of peeled carrot or peeled daikon, approximately 6 inches (152 mm) in length, and make a series of incisions running the length of the vegetable,* *all around the circumference; the fatter the daikon or carrot, the easier it is to make the incisions. Slice the vegetable thin and hold the slices in ice water until ready to use. Carrots may be blanched in boiling salted water, if desired; the daikon should be left raw.*

SPIKED BEET STEM

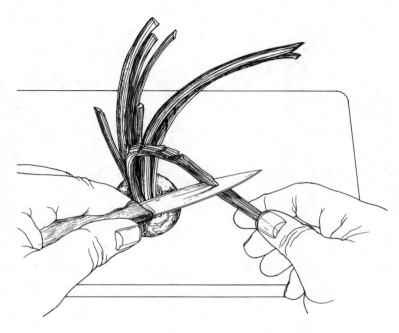

Remove the green leaves from the tops of the stems and make a series of 45-degree, angled incisions into the beet stems, approximately two-thirds of the way through the stem. The space between these incisions can vary depending on how much curl you wish to see in the stems—the closer the incisions, the tighter the curl. The stems can also be split lengthwise if they are more than ¼ inch (6 mm) thick. Place the cut stems in ice water to allow them to curl.

TIP *The stems can be left attached to the beet and used as an unusual centerpiece, or removed and used as separate circular garnishes (see color photo).*

Assorted pansies (carrot, butternut squash); assorted zinnias (butternut squash [rounded leaves], golden beets [rounded and pointed leaves]); assorted dahlias (pointed leaves: white turnip, rutabaga); Carrot Spears; Daikon Spears.

(Clockwise from bottom left)—
Mushroom Imprints; Radish
Lanterns; Celery Loops.

The vegetable cuts (top to bottom)—yellow and white turnips cut into losanges (diamonds) and arranged in a floral pattern; carrot sliced on the bias (yin-yang style); Vichy-style sliced carrot.

(Clockwise from left)—Spiked Leek Leaves; Zucchini Aster; zucchini cups.

(Clockwise from top left)—Twisted Cucumber Slices; Twisted Lemon Slices; Cucumber Sushi Garnish; Onion Begonia.

Red Jalapeño Daisies (two variations); Daikon Vegetable Cups (two variations).

(Clockwise from left)—Two watermelons: one with rose and leaf motif, the second with leaf top above a diamond pattern; fluted melon wedges (honeydew, cantaloupe); watermelon leaves; honeydew crown filled with cantaloupe parisienne; five-petal cantaloupe filled with watermelon parisienne.

(Top to bottom)—Fluted Cucumber Socle (filled with rolled, pickled ginger); Red Pepper Collars (holding blanched green string beans); cherry tomatoes (filled with herb cream cheese and garnished with thin half-circles of radish).

Tomato Roses; Cucumber Loops and Fans.

(Clockwise from top left)—Yellow Jalapeño Daisy; radish flower; Daikon Celestial Cube; radish flower.

(Clockwise from top left)—Red Onion Cups (filled with corn relish); Squash Drums (filled with carrot salad and green pea salad); Cucumber Timbales (scooped-out crowns, filled with radish salsa).

(Clockwise from top)—White Turnip Rose; Spiked Beet Stem; Radish Wheels; Celery Bundles tied with blanched leek greens.

(Clockwise from top left)—Rococo Apple; Pineapple Christmas Tree (inverted pineapple leaf top); Red Apple Feather; Bartlett Pear Feather.

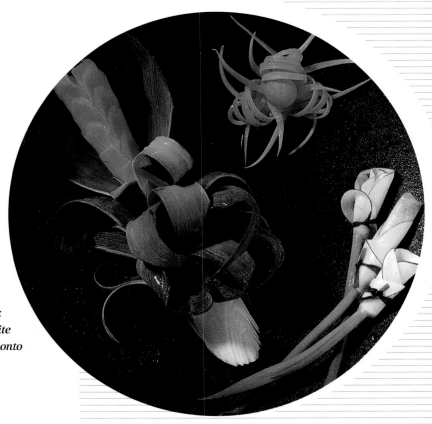

(Clockwise from left)— Leek Bromeliad Blossom; Carrot Spider Mum; White Turnip Calla Lilies (tied onto scallion greens).

Beet and carrot flowers embellishing the outer edge of a platter of crudités; there is a beet spur atop the crudité sauce (on left). The edge of the Brie is decorated with thin-sliced cucumber halves interspersed with small, round slices of radish. The loose center arrangement (unanchored) is made up of heirloom tomatoes (pear-shaped miniatures and "Sweet 100's"), a few blanched string beans, and some scallion greens.

(Counterclockwise from left)— Watermelon rind "bowl" filled with golden bing cherries, blackberries, blueberries, and sliced strawberries; orange honeydew melon wedges, sliced green honeydew melon, sliced watermelon. sliced pineapple, carved half papaya; watermelon with rose and leaf motif.

Bell Pepper

BELL PEPPER BASKET

Choose peppers that are blemish-free, though peppers with unusual shapes can yield unexpected shapes and forms. It is fairly easy to create a basket with a single looped-over handle, but a three- or four-part handle adds a little more interest. The key is to visualize the basket first, then execute the incisions. Bell peppers come in a variety of colors and shapes, and they tend to mature with three or four sections delineated by a group of mounds at the bottom. By following the contours of these sections on the side, you can create a handle with multiple sections. You effectively remove three or four segments, leaving a handle behind. The horizontal edge of the basket is cut roughly 1 to 1½ inches (26 to 38 mm) from the bottom of the pepper; it can be either a smooth incision or a zigzag (cook's choice applies).

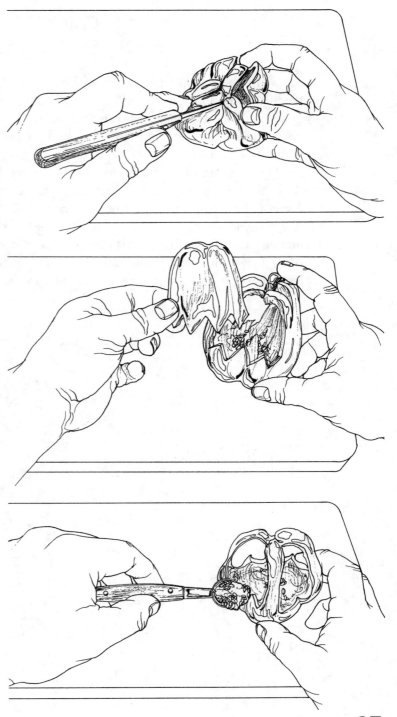

Carrot

CARROT
BROMELIAD BLOSSOM

Cut into the side of a peeled carrot at an angle of approximately 30 degrees, beginning at the top (the fat end). Make a second cut just above the first incision at a slightly steeper angle, releasing a small sliver of carrot. Repeat this step three times around the diameter of the carrot, then repeat the row of four petals all the way down the carrot.

Slice off and discard the root end of a large leek. Using a pair of scissors, trim the ends of the leaves lengthwise, parallel to the trunk of the leek. Trim away and discard any wilted or damaged leaves and rinse thoroughly in cold water. Using a paring knife, cut through the crease in the folds of the leaves, separating them into single panels. Place in ice water to allow them to curl. When ready to use, insert the thin end of the cut carrot down into the center of the leek, pressing it in firmly. Use as a garnish for large platters.

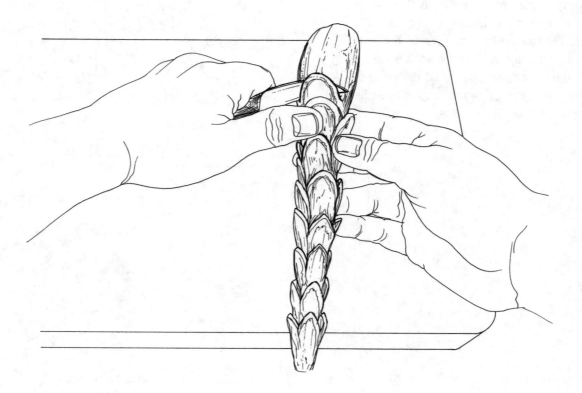

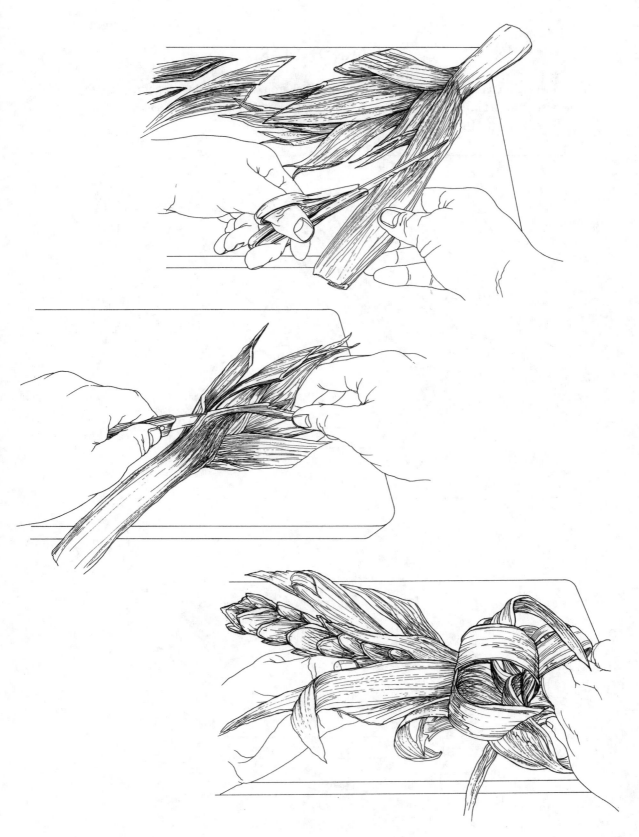

CARROT STAR

Using a channel knife, cut a series of parallel grooves, fairly close together, lengthwise into a fat, peeled carrot. Cut the carrot into $\frac{1}{16}$-inch (1-mm) slices and use them as part of a vegetable medley.

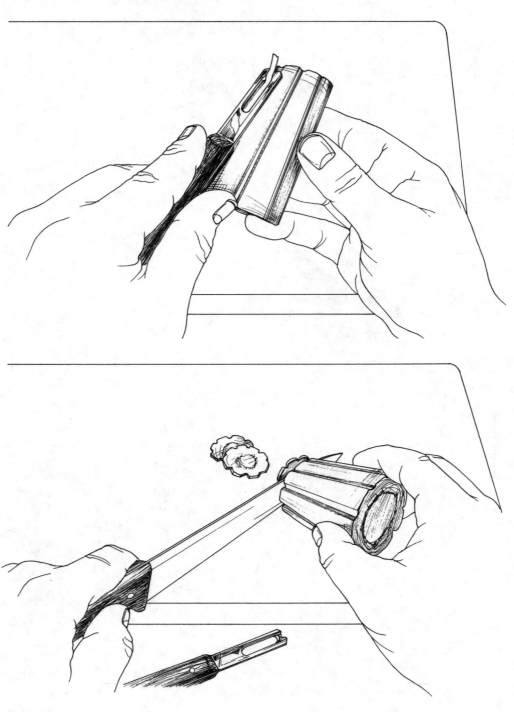

CARROT CACTUS FLOWER

Choose carrots as fat as available and peel them. Remove the end of the carrot—if it is thin at one end—leaving a carrot at least 6 inches (152 mm) long. Make a vertical incision about ¼ inch (6 mm) deep into the side of the carrot, running the full length of the carrot. Make a second incision about ⅛ inch (3 mm) ahead of the first cut at a slightly different angle, so that when it intersects with the bottom of the first cut, a small strip of carrot is released. Repeat this pair of cuts all around the circumference of the carrot.

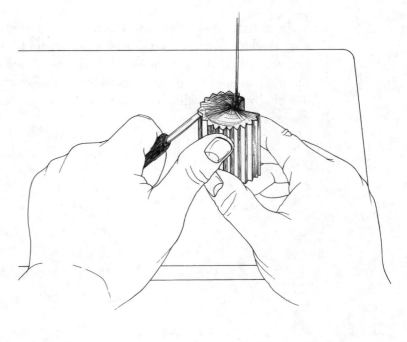

Trim the narrow end of the carrot into a cone at an angle of approximately 30 degrees. Insert an 8-inch (203-mm) bamboo skewer at the center of the cone and gently push it into the carrot about 2 or 3 inches (50 to 75 mm). It is important that this skewer be placed as close to the center as possible. Set the side of the blade of a paring knife on the surface of the cone, with the tip of the knife set against the skewer. Make a continuous cut around the cone, just past a full circle, shaving a thin layer of carrot. Remove the carrot cone and set in ice water. Push the skewer ¼ inch (6 mm) farther into the carrot before cutting the next cone.

Once you reach a comfortable level of competence with this technique, try making three complete turns instead of just one. Remove the resulting spiral and gently turn the two ends back into themselves, creating a double cone.

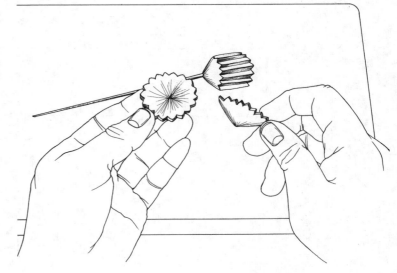

TIP PLEASE WORK SLOWLY AND CAREFULLY—*the carrot is a considerably harder material than daikon or cucumber, and slips can precipitate injuries.*

This flower form can be created with daikon radish and cucumber.

CARROT SPEAR

On a mandoline or electric slicer, slice a peeled carrot lengthwise ⅛ inch (3 mm) thick or less. Stack the slices together and trim with a paring knife, creating two pointed petals on each side, a point at the top, and a flat plane about 1 inch (26 mm) wide at the bottom. Using a bird's-beak knife, cut an additional three to five oval openings within each slice; make each opening pointed at each end. Place in ice water until ready to use.

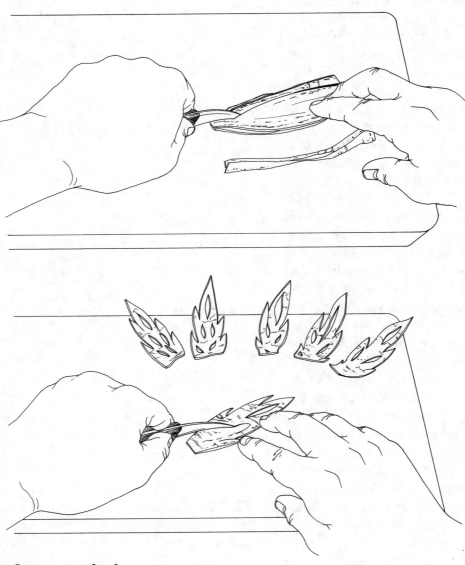

TIP *Carrot Spears can also be made with sliced daikon radish.*

CARROT ZINNIA I

Cut a peeled, fat carrot into segments 1½ to 2 inches (38 to 50 mm) long. Cut one of the segments with a five-rounded-petal metal cutter. Cut this into three pieces, each ½ inch (13 mm) long. Lightly mark the surface of the carrot with a paring knife, delineating the five petals. Shave the surface of each of the five petals at an angle so that a multilevel pattern is created. Repeat this cut on the opposite face, then cut the carrot piece in half; you should now have two flowers. Trim the bottom outside edge of each flower, making the edges thin and delicate. Place in ice water until needed. *Note:* Whether you choose the 1-inch (26-mm) cutter or the 1½-inch (38-mm) cutter will depend on the diameter of the carrot.

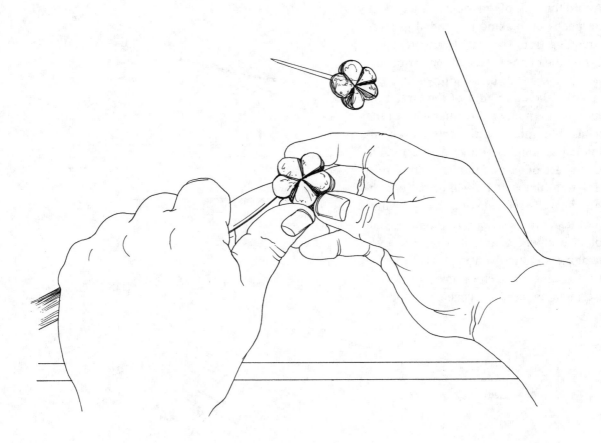

CARROT ZINNIA II

Cut a peeled, fat carrot into segments 1½ to 2 inches (38 to 50 mm) long. Cut one of the segments with a five-pointed-petal metal cutter. Cut this into three pieces, each ½ inch (13 mm) long. Using a small pois scoop, score a tiny circle in the center of each end of a segment. Using the point of a paring knife or bird's-beak knife, shave the surface of the carrot around the scored circle, angling in toward the base of the round center. Mark the petals by making five radial grooves extending from the round center. Repeat this on the opposite side of the carrot segment, then cut in half widthwise.

Trim the outer edge of the bottom of both pieces, making the outer edge of the petals thin and delicate. Now cut an additional triangular groove at the middle of the base of each of the five petals, running from the center circle up to roughly the center of each petal. Place in ice water until ready to use. *Note:* After cutting the initial segment of carrot using the five-petal metal cutter, you may wish to slice it into coins ¹⁄₁₆ inch (1 mm) thick and use them as part of a vegetable medley.

TIP *Any of the other shapes of cutters—pointed petals, notched petals, or scalloped edge—can be used; each will yield a slightly different shape of flower.*

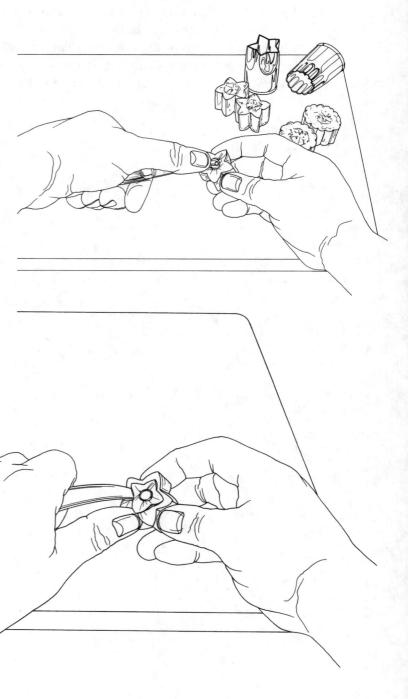

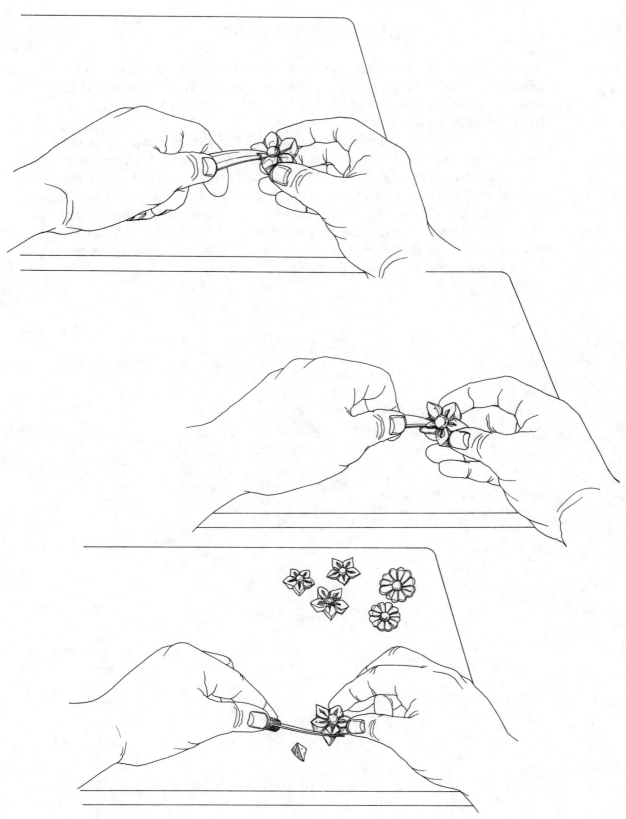

CARROT SPIDER MUM

Choose a fat carrot with as little taper as possible. Peel the carrot, trim the ends, then cut it to a length of approximately 6 inches (152 mm). Slice the carrot lengthwise on an electric slicer or mandoline to a thickness of $\frac{1}{16}$ inch (1 mm) or less. (It must be thin enough to roll without cracking.)

Trim two slices into a clean rectangle. Make an incision beginning $\frac{1}{2}$ inch (13 mm) from one end and $\frac{1}{8}$ inch (3 mm) from one side, moving down the slices and toward the outside edge. It should exit the outside edge within an inch of the opposite end. Repeat this process on the opposing side, then twice on the opposite end. You should now see four long, pointed strips coming off the sides, slightly overlapped. Make another two or three parallel incisions in the center of the slices, running $\frac{1}{2}$ inch (13 mm) from each end and $\frac{1}{16}$ inch (1 mm) apart. These cuts in the center area of the carrot will remain close-ended.

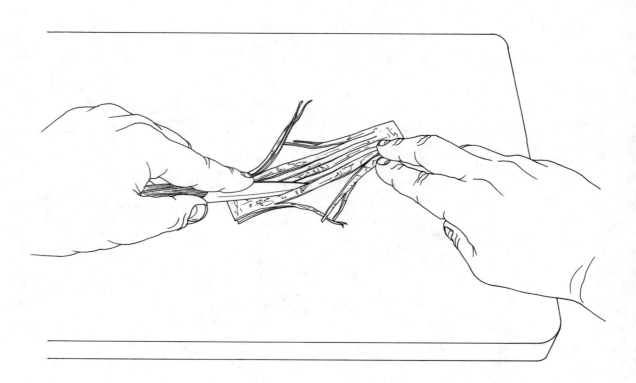

Prepare a small cylindrical slice of carrot measuring ¼ by ¾ inch (6 to 19 mm) and insert a toothpick through its center. Take one of the slices of carrot and turn the ends sideways toward each other and then set them over one another. Skewer this onto the toothpick and down onto the small slice. Repeat with the second slice, skewering it on top of and opposite the first slice. Anchor the slices with a small carrot sphere (cut with the noisette end of a parisienne scoop). Place in ice water until ready to use.

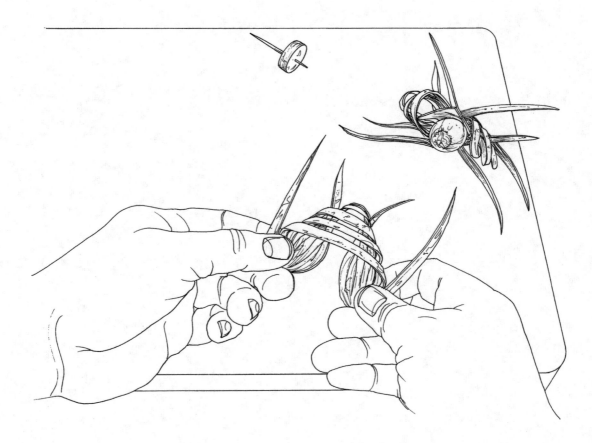

TIP *This flower can also be prepared with daikon.*

Celery

CELERY BRUSH

Cut a large celery stalk into segments approximately 3 inches (75 mm) long. Square these segments off so that they measure approximately ½ inch (13 mm) wide and ¼ inch (6 mm) thick. Make a series of very fine parallel incisions running up to about ¼ inch (6 mm) from one end of the segment. These incisions should be $\frac{1}{16}$ inch (1 mm) thick or less. Place in ice water to allow the strips to curl.

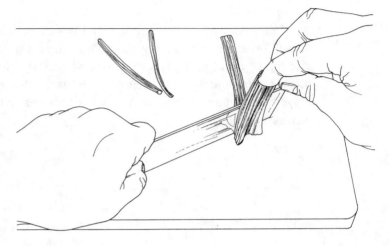

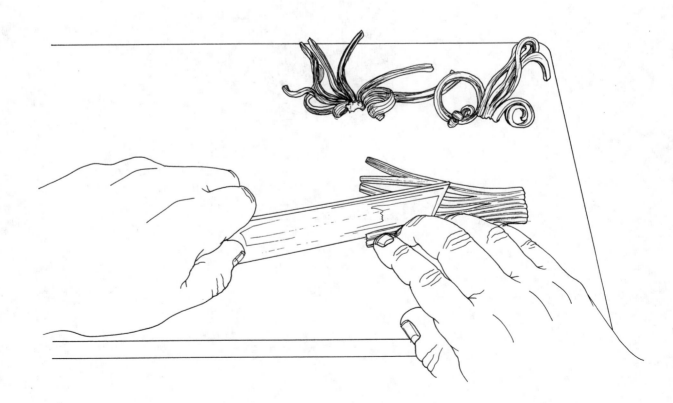

CELERY ROSE

Cut a thin slice off the very bottom of a stalk of celery and discard. Cut off the bottom "butt" of the celery to approximately 3 inches (75 mm). Trim any blemishes from the exterior, then rinse. Make a cut into the outside of each external piece of celery stalk. These cuts should be thin at the top, becoming slightly thicker toward the bottom.

Using a bird's-beak knife, cut the top of each stalk at a 45-degree angle toward the center of the celery and remove the cut piece. Cutting at this angle makes the top edges of each stalk more or less curved; trim as needed any that are not. Repeat this process with each stalk on each subsequent row until all the stalks have been trimmed. Place in ice water until ready to use and to allow the outer leaves to curl.

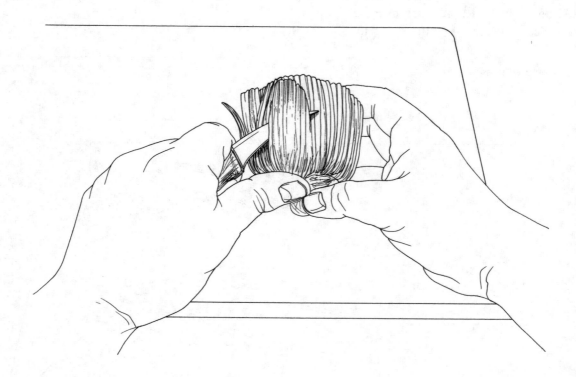

TIP *This garnish can also be created on the bottom ends of bok choy, a crunchy vegetable with dark green leaves used extensively in Chinese-American cooking. The technique is similar, although the step creating an external row of petals can be eliminated.*

Cucumber

CUCUMBER FAN AND LOOPS

Hothouse cucumbers are the best variety to sculpt because they contain fewer seeds than the standard supermarket variety and are not coated with fat or paraffin.

Cut a 3-inch (75-mm) segment from one end of a cucumber and place it, cut surface down, on a cutting surface. Make a vertical cut down through this piece, approximately one fourth of the way across its width. Tip the smaller piece over so that it is lying on the cutting surface. Remove a triangular piece by making a 20-degree angled cut. Make five parallel incisions, about 1/32 inch (1/2 mm) apart, to within 1/4 inch (6 mm) of the top of the piece. Run the fifth incision through the entire piece so that it is severed. The fan is made by simply pressing down and to one side so that the slices fan out.

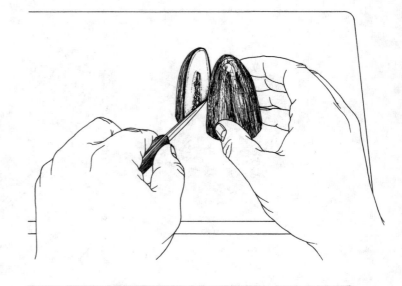

For the loops, turn the second and fourth interior slices over and down into the crevice at the base of each slice. Press them gently into this crevice to hold them in place. *Note:* For the fan, you may cut as many slices as you wish. For the loops, you may wish to make three, five, or seven parallel incisions; the three-slice loop works quite well as a border.

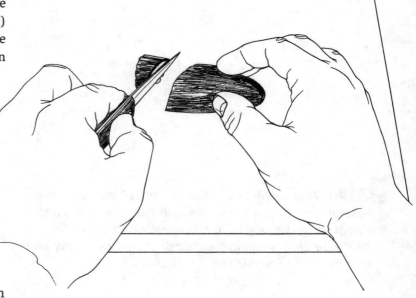

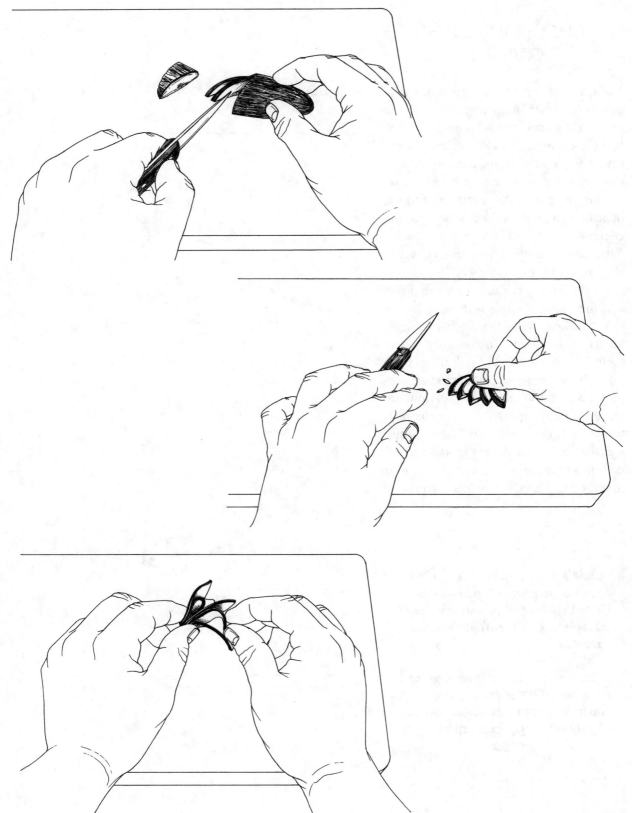

CUCUMBER SUSHI GARNISH

Cut a segment of cucumber 2½ to 3 inches (63 to 75 mm) long and make an incision at its center down about halfway. Make a 45-degree, angled incision in the center of one side, cutting halfway through the segment, then remove that wedge. Repeat this cut on the reverse side in the opposing angle. If desired, scoop out the cucumber flesh and seeds using a parisienne scoop. Store briefly in ice water until ready to use.

This garnish can also be created two at a time from a single segment 3 inches (75 mm) long. Make the same 45-degree, angled incisions into the side of the segment. Make another vertical incision through the center of the cucumber, running from end to end of the previous incisions. Gently separate the two pieces. If they do not easily separate, carefully run a paring knife over the cut surfaces a second time to make certain that all incisions intersect; this method avoids waste.

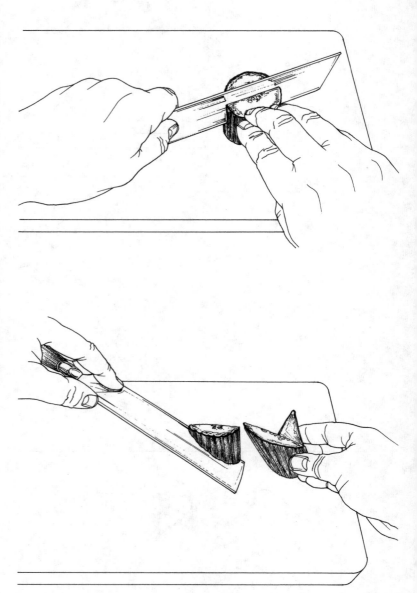

TIP *The sides of this garnish can be "feathered," though the small space will permit only about three wedges; see Apple Feather, page 120.*

This cut can be used on a great number of other food items, including apple, banana, lemon, hard-boiled egg, and radish.

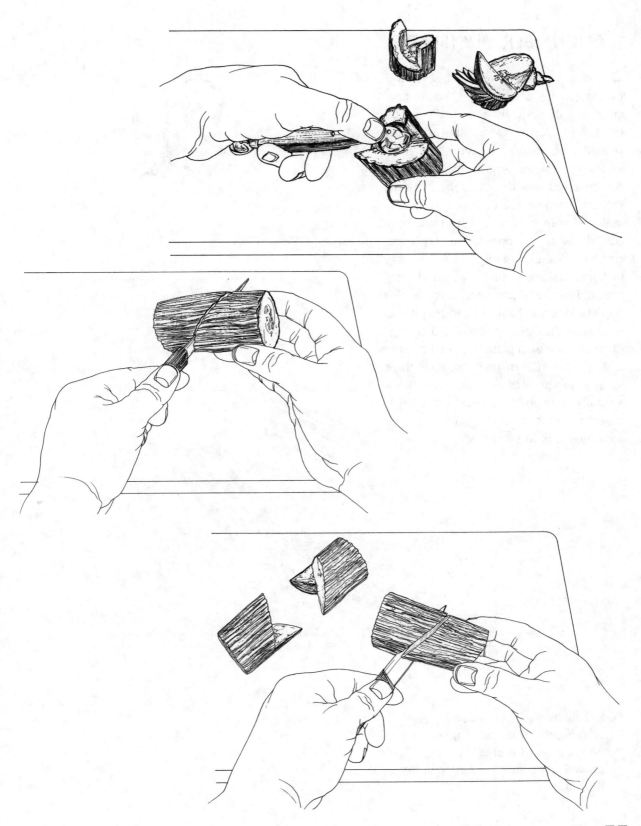

CUCUMBER LILY (FLAT)

Stand a cucumber segment, 2½ to 3 inches (63 to 75 mm) long, on its end, cut it in half vertically, then make a third cut to remove the seeds. Repeat on the second half, if needed. With a channel knife, cut a series of grooves lengthwise on the exterior of the cucumber. Lay the section down on the cutting surface and make a ¹⁄₁₆-inch (1-mm) cut at one end, cutting as far as possible into the cucumber without going all the way through. Make a second ¹⁄₁₆-inch (1-mm) cut and remove the slice. Repeat this process until you have six half-round butterflied slices. Open each one and arrange three of them on a plate or platter around a single point, then place another three slices over those three. *Note:* This is essentially a two-dimensional flower that must be arranged on the plate or platter on which it is to be served.

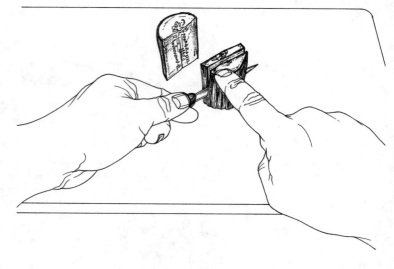

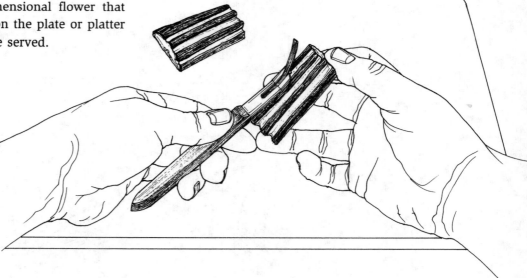

TIP *For variety, consider eight- or ten-petal flowers—four or five petals around a single point, topped with another four or five on top.*

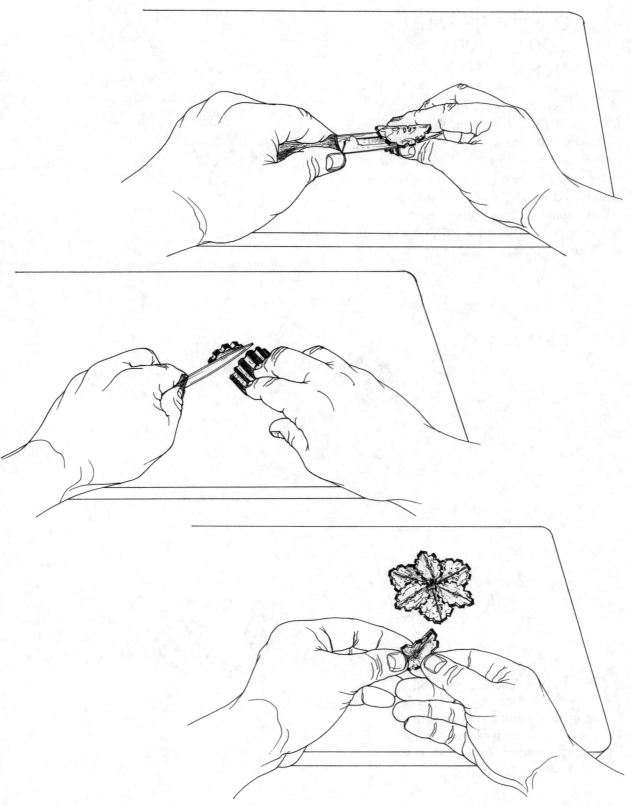

CUCUMBER TIMBALE I (ZIGZAG WITH CHANNELS)

Trim approximately ½ inch (13 mm) from the end of a cucumber; then, using a channel knife, make a series of parallel grooves down the length of the segment, spaced about ⅛ inch (3 mm) apart. Scoop out the center seeds with a parisienne scoop, about halfway down into the piece. Store in ice water briefly, or wrap in a damp paper towel and refrigerate.

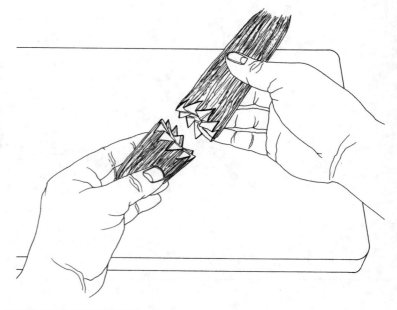

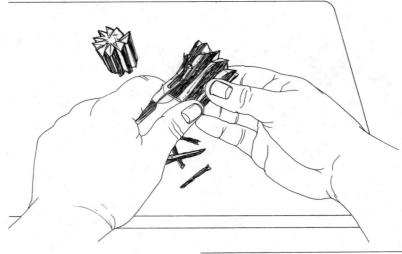

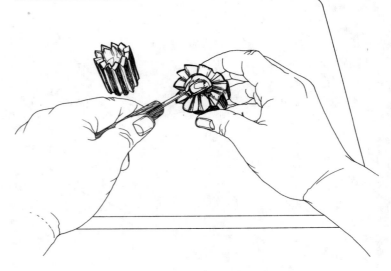

TIP *Timbales are a form of socle—a container for food made out of food—and they can be used to serve a small portion of relish, chutney, pickle, mayonnaise sauce, and so on.*

CUCUMBER TIMBALE II (SCALLOPED EDGE)

Cut a segment of hothouse cucumber, 2½ to 3 inches (63 to 75 mm) long, with a scallop-edged metal cutter. Discard the exterior. Cut the segment in half on a slight bias—about 30 degrees. Scoop out the center seeds, and discard; store until ready to use. *Note:* This particular timbale makes an excellent socle for an hors d'oeuvre. Be sure to make it small enough so that when filled—with, for example, a poached shrimp and a little wasabi-flavored cocktail sauce—it consists of a single bite. This may mean cutting the segments closer to 2 inches (50 mm) than to 2½ inches (63 mm).

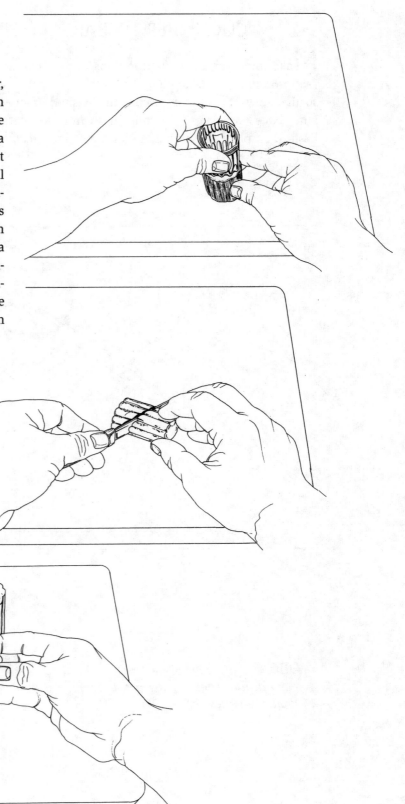

CUCUMBER TIMBALE III (THREE-PETAL)

Make three vertical radial incisions into a cucumber segment 2½ to 3 inches (75 to 63 mm) long, dividing it into three sections. Shave the top of the sections so that they are rounded. Make an incision about ¼ inch (6 mm) in from the outer edge to separate the inner flesh from the petals. Remove and discard the flesh, then place the timbale in ice water until ready to use.

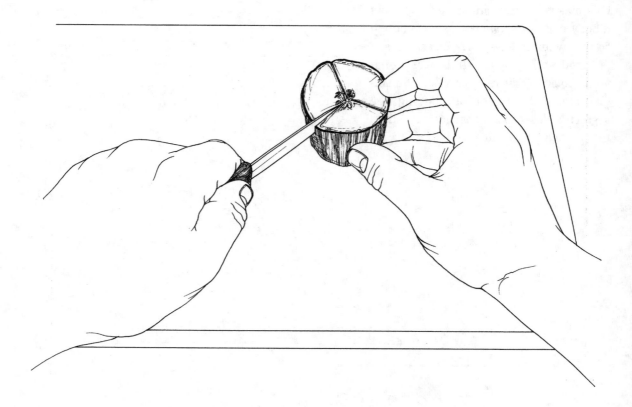

TIP *A fine zigzag pattern can be cut into the edges of the petals for added complexity.*

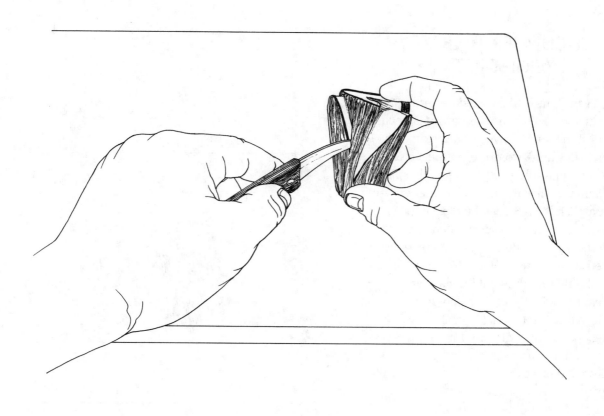

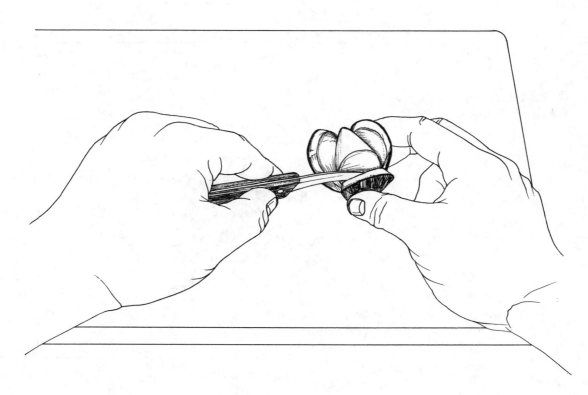

CUCUMBER TIMBALE IV
(EIGHT-PETAL)

Make four vertical incisions through the center of a cucumber segment 3 inches (75 mm) long, down to approximately 1 inch (26 mm) from the bottom, creating eight equal wedges. (Four equally spaced diametric lines through the center will accomplish this.) Shave the tops of the eight petals so that they are rounded. Cut down vertically into the timbale to create eight petals, roughly ¼ inch (6 mm) thick. Make two or three additional vertical incisions—as thin as possible—down into each petal. Scoop out and discard the remaining center seeds and flesh and place the timbale in ice water to allow the petals to curl outward.

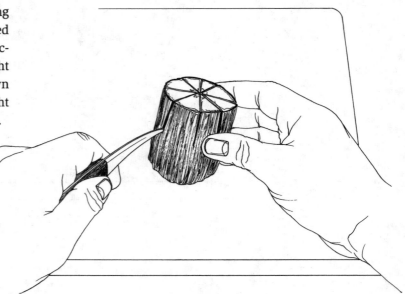

TIP *This flower can also be made with five or six petals.*

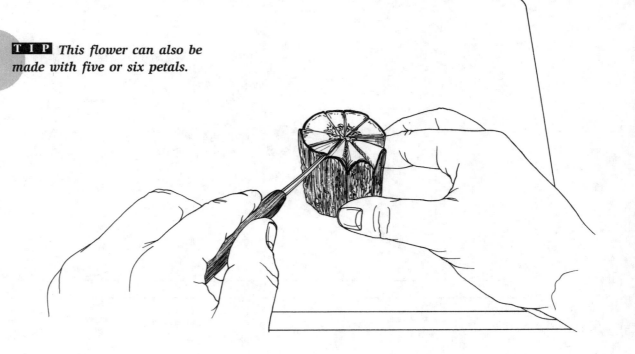

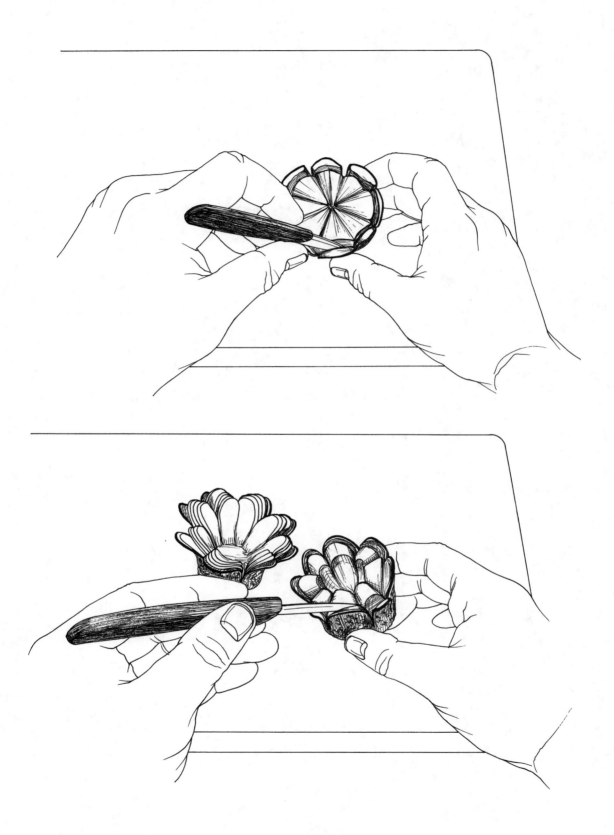

Daikon

DAIKON BUTTER CUP

Peel a daikon and cut it into segments 3 inches (75 mm) long. Cut each one using a large, five-rounded-petal metal cutter. Make five 45-degree, angled cuts at one end to create the outside edges of the five round petals. Form the petals by making an incision that begins at the top of each of these five shapes and continues down into the center of the daikon. Twist the flower off, then pierce it with a toothpick, placing a small sphere of carrot, zucchini, or other vegetable inside of the flower. Place in ice water until ready to use.

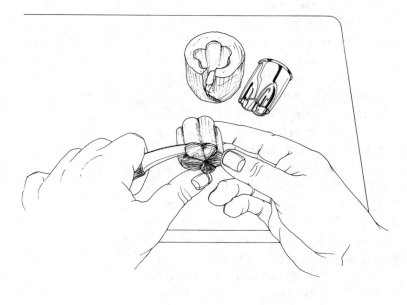

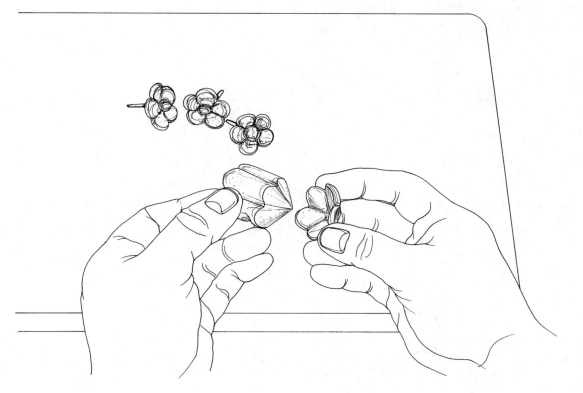

DAIKON CELESTIAL CUBE

Cut a daikon cube to roughly 1½ inches (38 mm) square per side. Set a paring knife over the center of one plane. Tilt the knife 45 degrees to one side and make an incision about 3/16 inch (4 mm) deep. Angle the knife in the opposite direction and make a second incision 3/16 inch (4 mm) deep. Reposition the knife at a right angle to the first line and repeat the two 3/16-inch (4-mm) incisions. The total number of incisions is now four.

Repeat the process, this time making two incisions from corner to corner, then another two across the opposite corners. There should now be eight wedgelike pieces ready to remove. If any of these wedges are not fully severed, run your knife gently over the incisions again. Repeat this process on the remaining five surface planes of the cube, then place in ice water until ready to use.

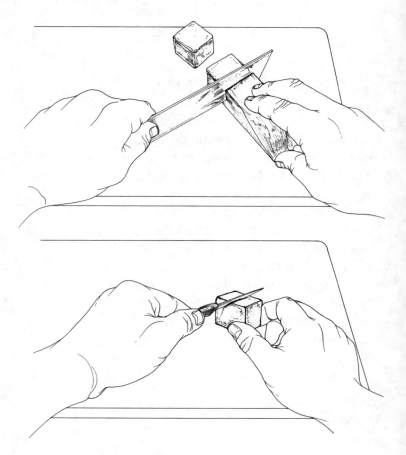

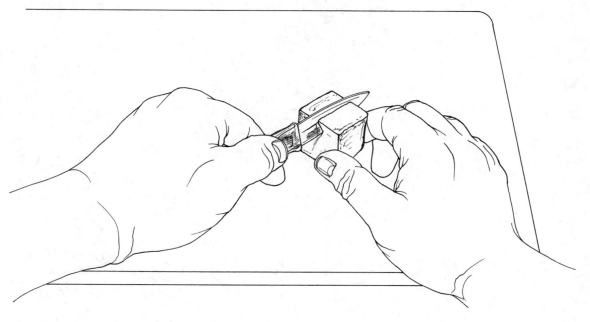

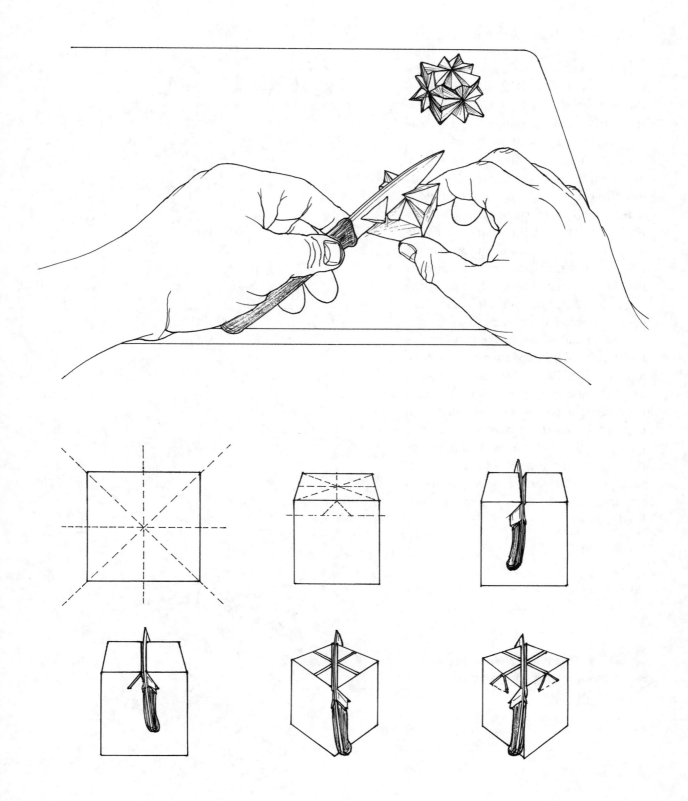

DAIKON FOUR-PETAL CUP

Make four 30-degree, angled cuts at the bottom (the thin end) of a daikon, leaving four flat planes; these will be the outside surfaces of the flower. Repeat these cuts, beginning each at the top of each of the flat planes; make the top of each petal very thin, then cut down, angling slightly, into the center of the daikon in order to make the base of each petal gradually thicker. Bring each incision down only about three fourths of the way into the daikon. Twist the flower off, then reshave the four outside planes to adjust the angle. Repeat as needed. Place the flowers in ice water until ready to use.

Additional staggered rows of petals can be added by repeating the process. Simply cut a flat surface between each petal of the previous row, then cut again to make four petals. This double-rowed cup can be carefully twisted off at this point, or the rows can be continued all the way up the vegetable without separating the flowers. It can then be used in arrangements or split lengthwise and used cut-side down.

TIP *This same flower can also be created with cucumber and zucchini.*

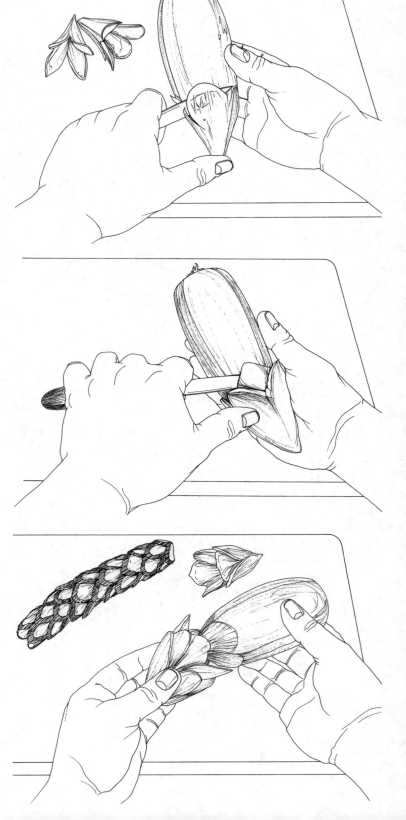

DAIKON FIVE-PETAL CUP

Peel a daikon, then cut five flat planes on the root end (the thin end) at an angle of approximately 20 degrees. Cut five petals, beginning each on one of the edges created by the planes; this is completely different from the Four-Petal Cup on the previous page. Twist the flower off, reshave the five planes, then continue cutting the flowers as needed. If necessary, you may wish to trim each of the petals to a sharp point, using a pair of scissors or a sharp knife.

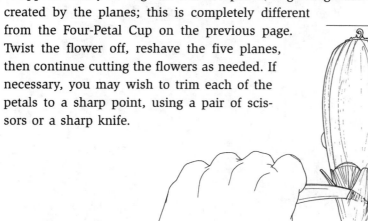

DAIKON STAIRS

Slice the thin end of a peeled, fat daikon at a 45-degree angle. Using three or four long bamboo skewers, prop up the daikon so that the plane of the cut surface rests flat on the cutting surface and the daikon is fairly stable. Slice the top so that it is horizontal, then make a 1-inch vertical incision at a right angle. Make another horizontal incision to intersect with the vertical cut and remove that piece of daikon. Repeat this pattern all the way down the daikon, following the curves of the vegetable as you see fit. Place in ice water until ready to use.

This rather unusual creation lends a kind of whimsical presence to the dinner or buffet table. Use it on a platter surrounded by crudités, cold cuts, or even antipasti. For a variation, cut two sets of stairs, side by side, on the same daikon.

TIP *This garnish can also be created using a hothouse cucumber.*

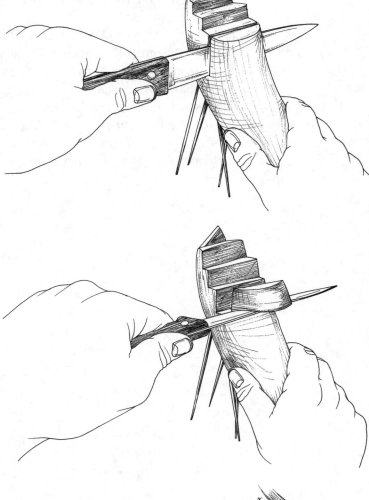

Jalapeño

JALAPEÑO DAISY

Slice off the very end tip of a red or green jalapeño. Using a bird's-beak knife, make a series of parallel incisions, about ⅛ inch (3 mm) apart, from the stem end of the pepper down through the snipped end.

From the snipped end, cut down into the pepper, severing the flesh from the connective material on the interior. Excess pieces of this connective material can be discarded, but the seed stem in the center should stay in place—it will become part of the flower after the petals open. Place in ice water to open the petals.

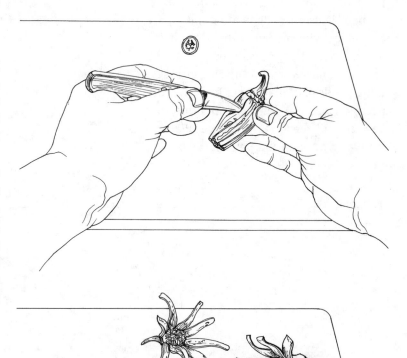

TIP *Be sure to wash your hands thoroughly and vigorously after cutting this flower; the capsicum compounds in the jalapeño can be extremely caustic, particularly to the eyes and mouth.*

JALAPEÑO TULIP

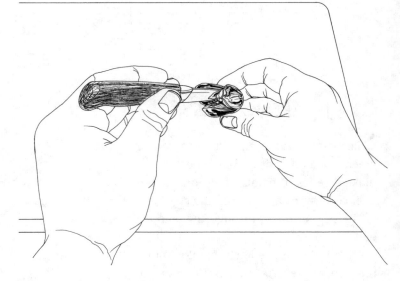

Make three equidistant incisions from the stem end down to the tip of the jalapeño. Make one or two additional *V*-shaped incisions (depending on space available) within each section, following the contour of the outside edge. As with the daisy, cut down into the pepper, severing the flesh of the pepper from the connective material on the interior but keeping the seed stem in place. Place in ice water to open the petals.

TIP *Be sure to wash your hands thoroughly and vigorously after cutting this flower; the capsicum compounds in the jalapeño can be extremely caustic, particularly to the eyes and mouth.*

JALAPEÑO
WILDFLOWER

This flower requires an exceptionally sharp paring or bird's-beak knife. Score a series of zigzag cuts around the circumference of the stem end. Be careful not to cut all the way through the pepper. Repeat this three or four times, depending on the size of the pepper, with each row of zigzags alternating with the row above it. Using the point of the knife, cut the skin of the jalapeño away from the flesh, following the outline of the small triangular forms created by the zigzag cuts. Repeat this technique with the other rows, then place the pepper in ice water to allow the skin to curl.

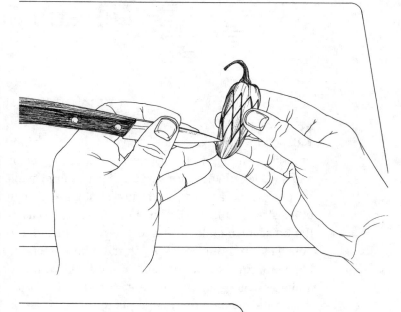

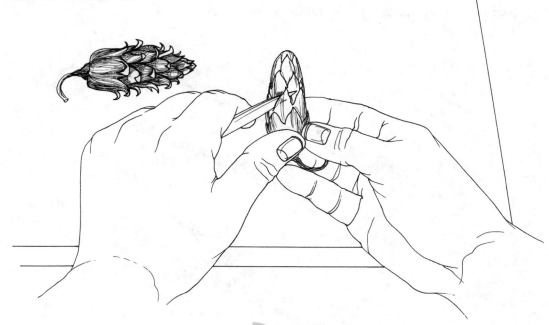

TIP *Be sure to wash your hands thoroughly and vigorously after cutting this flower; the capsicum compounds in the jalapeño can be extremely caustic, particularly to the eyes and mouth.*

Leek and Scallion

LEEK BRAID

Blanch the dark green leek leaves in boiling, salted water about a half minute or until limp enough to braid (be careful not to overcook). Drain, dip into cold water, and slice lengthwise into strips 1/8 inch (3 mm) wide. Place the ends of three strips on top of one another, each angled slightly outward, and tie together using another strip of blanched leaf. Lift one of the outside strips and lay it in between the adjacent middle strip and the other outside strip. Repeat this with the other outside strip, bringing it over in the other direction; repeat this process until completed. Secure the bottom end of the braid with another small strip of leek tied in a simple square knot; snip excess leek using a pair of scissors. Use braids as a decorative element on a large platter of food, around the edge of a whole cheese (such as a Brie or a rectangular piece of Swiss, Cheddar, Jack, etc.), or to wrap fish paupiettes (little packages), beef roulades, and so on.

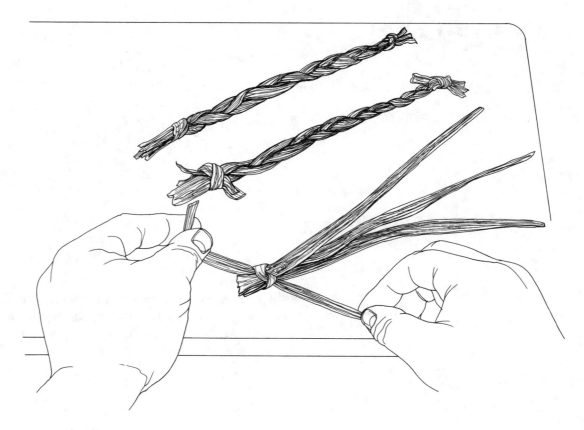

SPIKED LEEK LEAF

This garnish is similar to the cut-paper snowflakes that many of us made in grade school art class by folding small squares of paper into eighths, then rounding the edges and snipping small triangles from the edges to create an elaborate pattern. Because leek leaves are naturally folded in half, they can be cut in various ways, using a knife or scissors, then opened and used creatively. Experiment with cuts made at various angles. You may also wish to split the leaves lengthwise; when placed in ice water, they will curl in interesting ways.

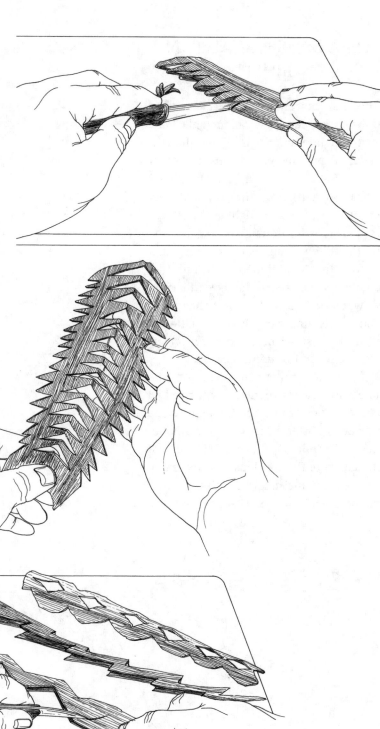

LEEK BRUSH/SCALLION BRUSH

Slice the root end from a leek and cut off the dark green leaves at an angle, leaving the white and light green bottom portion (save the green tops for other dishes). Split the leek in half, stopping 2 inches (50 mm) from the trimmed end. Repeat this split at a right angle to the first cut, creating four quarters. Run the tip of a knife through each quarter, making four to six additional incisions (depending on the size of the leek). Place in ice water to allow to curl. The brush makes a riveting garnish on a platter or as part of a small mukimono flower arrangement on a buffet table.

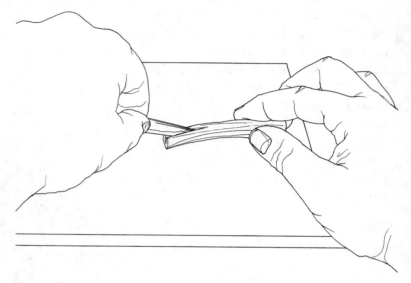

Scallion brushes are made in the same way, except that you will need to make only one or two additional incisions into each quarter, because of the smaller size. A Double Scallion Brush—an essential part of Peking Duck—is created by making these incisions in both ends of a scallion piece 3 inches (75 mm) long.

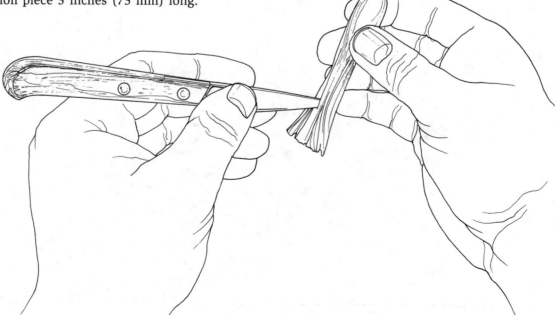

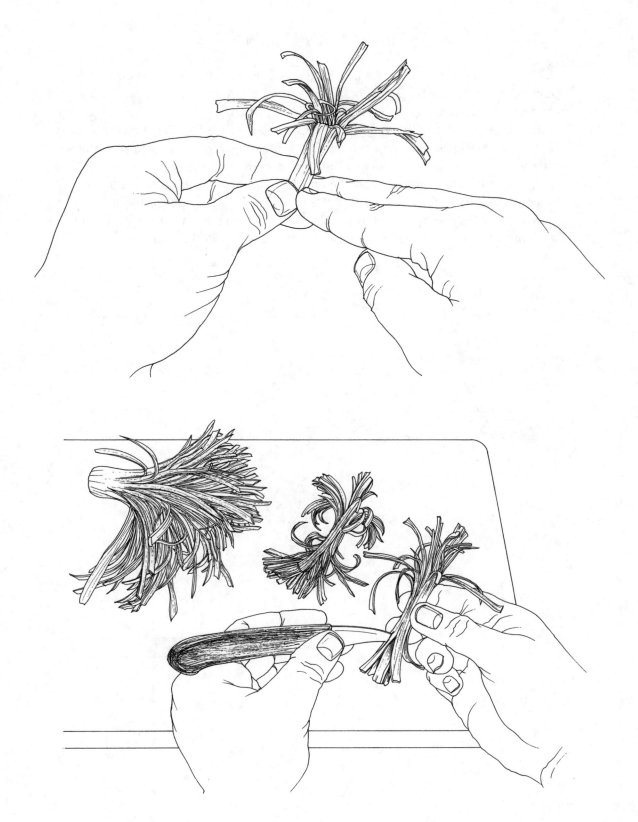

LEEK OR SCALLION TIE

Blanch dark green leek or scallion leaves in boiling, salted water about a half minute or until limp enough to braid (be careful not to overcook). Drain, dip in cold water, slice lengthwise into strips ¼ inch (6 mm) wide, and set aside. Lay two lengths of leaf on a working surface, parallel, about 1½ inches (38 mm) apart. Cut lightly blanched julienned vegetables (such as asparagus, bell pepper, carrot, celery, string beans, turnip, and so on) to lengths of approximately 3 inches (75 mm). Set a bundle of these across the two ties. Lift the ends of one tie and make a simple overhand turn. Tug so that the julienned bundle is pulled together securely. Tie a second knot on top (this will effectively create a square knot) and trim the ends with a knife or scissors. Tie the second strip the same way.

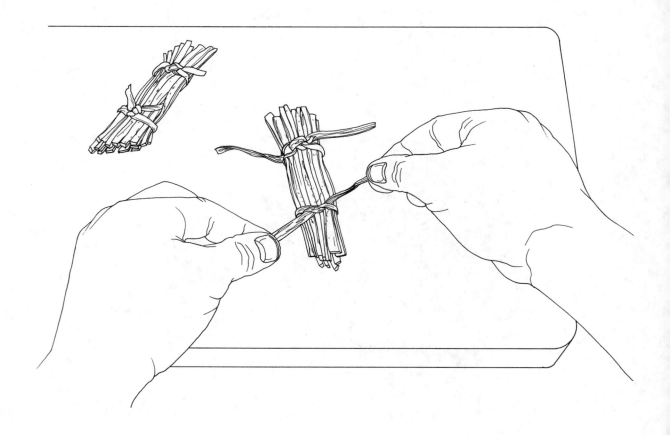

SCALLION VARIATIONS

The long, green stems of scallions can be cut lengthwise into two or three long strips, which when placed in ice water can yield visually pleasing shapes. When cut widthwise into $\frac{1}{8}$ to $\frac{1}{4}$ inch (3 to 6 mm) pieces—the bias angle should be as sharp as 15 degrees—because the stems are hollow, a number of elongated elliptical loops will result. Make an incision at one end of these loops, and it will spring open, appearing like two leaves on the stem of a flower. Both the intact loops and the cut ones can be used in innovative ways (see Brie cheese color photo).

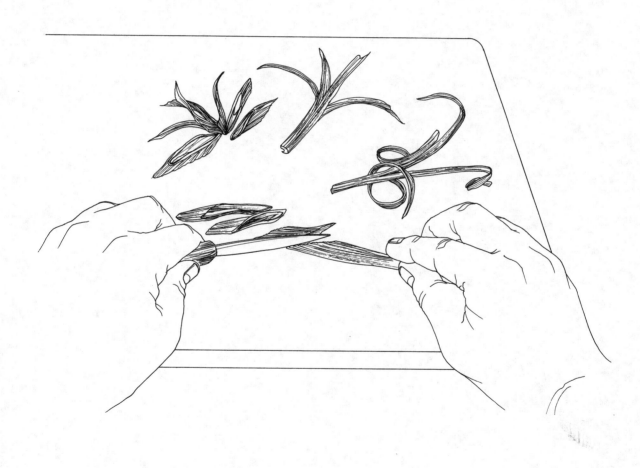

Mushrooms

MUSHROOM IMPRINTS

This technique works best with large, very fresh mushrooms. Simply press the tip of a paring knife down into the top of the mushroom, slightly away from and pointed toward the center top. This will create a small triangular arrow pointed toward the top of the mushroom. Repeat this step, creating a second arrow adjacent the first one, then continue until a row is completed. If the mushroom is large enough, a second, third, and sometimes a fourth row can be added. The mushroom must be brushed liberally with lemon juice in order to prevent it from turning brown.

The possible variations in pattern here are endless. For example, perform the same technique with the knife pointed away from the center. Or try a pair of arrows, each facing away from the center, in four different directions. Turn the knife around—toward the center— and highlight the four pairs or marks from the opposite directions. *Note:* If an imprinted mushroom is to be used as a garnish for a mushroom omelet, poached fish, or grilled steak, it should be poached in a lemon bath or dry white wine first. Be aware, however, that the imprint will lose some of its definition in the process of poaching.

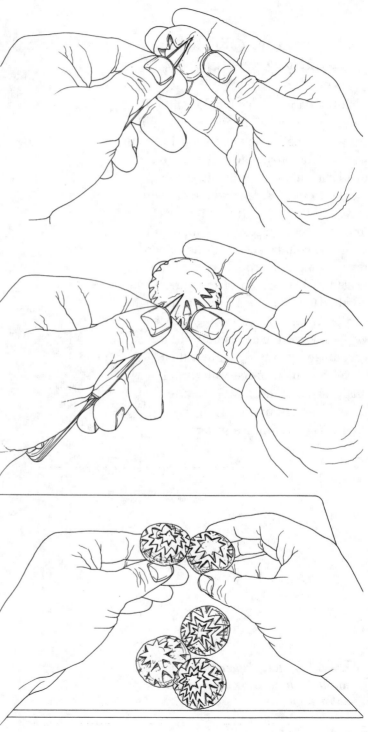

ONION CHRYSANTHEMUM

Slice a large, peeled onion into two halves, not quite all the way down to the core—the halves should remain connected by approximately ¼ inch (6 mm) of uncut onion. Repeat this cut perpendicular to the first, again down to within a ¼ inch (6 mm) of the bottom, yielding four quarters. Repeat two more times, each cut equidistant from the previous, resulting in eight equal wedges all connected at the bottom of the core. Make another four incisions through the eight sections, creating a total of sixteen wedges. Press the petals outward to encourage them to open, and then place the onion in ice water until ready to use. The flower may require some coaxing to open, even after it is placed in ice water.

TIP *A sharp zigzag will yield another interesting faux mum (see color photo).*

ONION CUP

Cut a zigzag around the circumference of a medium to large red, white, or yellow peeled onion. Remove a ½-inch (12-mm)-thick slice from the bottom of each cut half and carefully separate the layers. Place a thin slice of carrot, turnip, or some other vegetable in the bottom, and use the cup as a socle for a relish, chutney, pickle, or mayonnaise sauce.

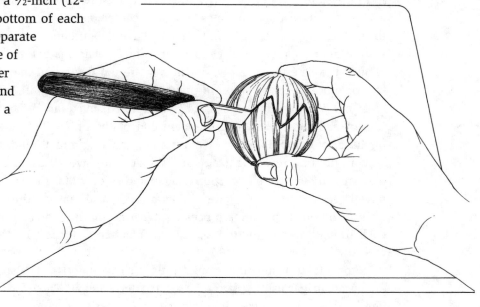

ONION ARTICHOKE

Because several layers of the onion are removed in the process of making this garnish, it is a good idea to start with a fairly large onion. Slice a very thin piece from the stem end of a red or yellow onion, then remove the outermost peel. Cut a zigzag pattern that emanates from the center of the stem end, cutting lightly through the first layer. It is important to have a light hand here, as the onion layers are only $1/16$ to $1/8$ inch (1 to 3 mm) thick. Incisions can always be carefully recut if they are too shallow, but if they are too deep, you may have to remove two or more layers of onion to prevent petals from falling off.

Once the first row of zigzags is completed, make an incision from the bottom of one zigzag down to the stem end of the onion, lightly scoring through one layer of onion. Pull that layer off and remove it from around the entire onion, leaving the first row of zigzag cuts. (Be sure to save all the usable onion parts that are removed for stock, soup, sauce, and so on.) Make sure all the petals that have been revealed are secure; if they are not, you may need to remove another layer of onion. Repeat this process, staggering the incisions so that the point of each triangle formed by the zigzag cut falls between the triangles of the previous row.

Store in ice water until ready to use. These onions can also be split in half and used to garnish a platter of roasted food items. They are also quite tasty lightly coated with olive oil, seasoned with a little salt and pepper, and roasted until tender and lightly caramelized.

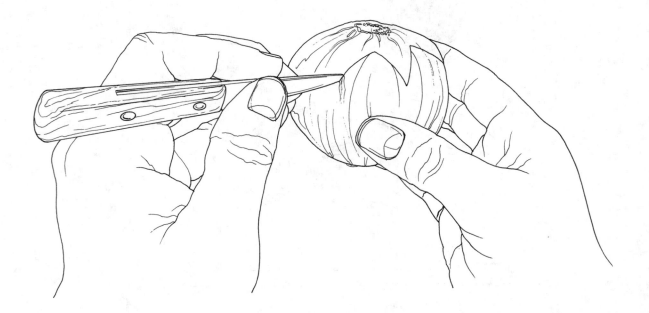

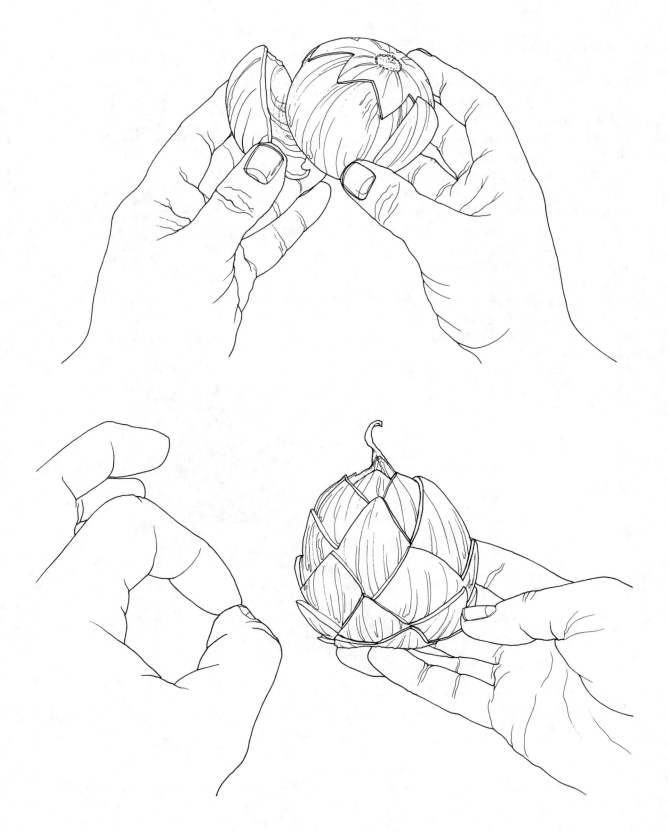

ONION STAR FLOWER

Cut a peeled, yellow onion around its core into eight equal wedges, then separate three of the wedges into individual curved slices. Take a small, round slice of daikon, approximately 1 by ¼ inch (26 by 6 mm) thick, and run a toothpick perpendicularly through its center. Impale one end of eight to ten of the curved slices onto the toothpick, concave side facing up. Position the wedges evenly in a circle to yield a symmetrical flower. Trim the toothpick to about ¼ inch (6 mm) in length and top with a small, black olive or ball cut from daikon. Spray with water and store covered in the refrigerator until ready to use.

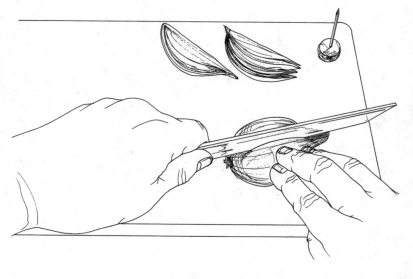

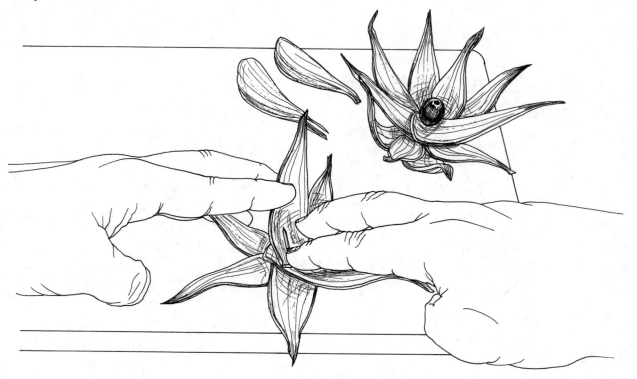

Radish

RADISH FAN AND MUM

Remove a thin slice from one side of a radish. Make a series of parallel incisions $1/16$ inch (1 mm) apart across the width of radish to within $1/4$ inch (6 mm) of the stem end. Press the radish down on its side so that the petals are slightly fanned out, then place in ice water to allow it to open further.

To create the mum, repeat the series of cuts across the radish, perpendicular to the first series. Place in ice water to allow the flower to open further.

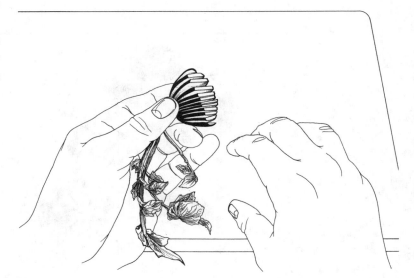

TIP *For aesthetic reasons, you may wish to allow the stems and leaves of the radish to remain in place. Be sure to trim them, removing any broken or damaged pieces, and to rinse thoroughly.*

TIP *Radishes are an excellent sculpting medium for several reasons: their color contrast—red exterior, white interior—their crisp texture, and the way they open in ice water.*

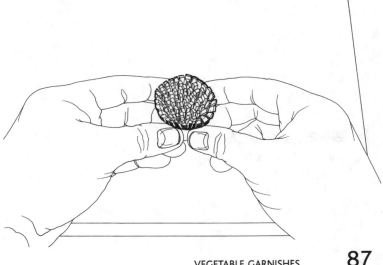

RADISH MUSHROOM

The mushroom form is best made on large, long radishes whose long, thin root is intact. Slice off and remove the leaves, then turn the radish over and lightly score it around its circumference, just above the midpoint. Invert it again and make a series of cuts from the outside edge of the top (where the leaves were) into the radish so as to intersect with the score line. Continue those cuts all around until a miniature mushroom shape is created.

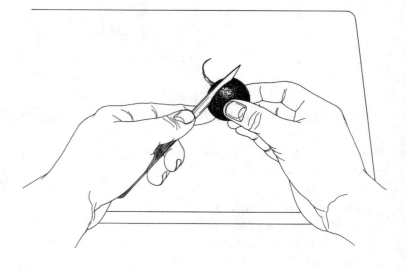

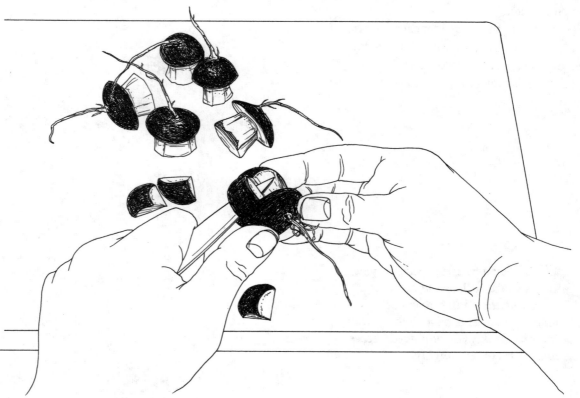

TIP *The long, thin root piece adds an interesting character to the top of the piece.*

RADISH ROSETTE I

Lightly shave the two ends of a radish, making it smooth and round. Cut a six-sided, star-shaped opening in one end, using a small *V*-shaped cutter. Using the same cutter or a bird's-beak knife, cut six vertical wedges into the side of the radish, beginning at the points between the angles created by the six-sided opening. Each of these wedges should remain attached at the bottom. Place in ice water to allow the wedges to open.

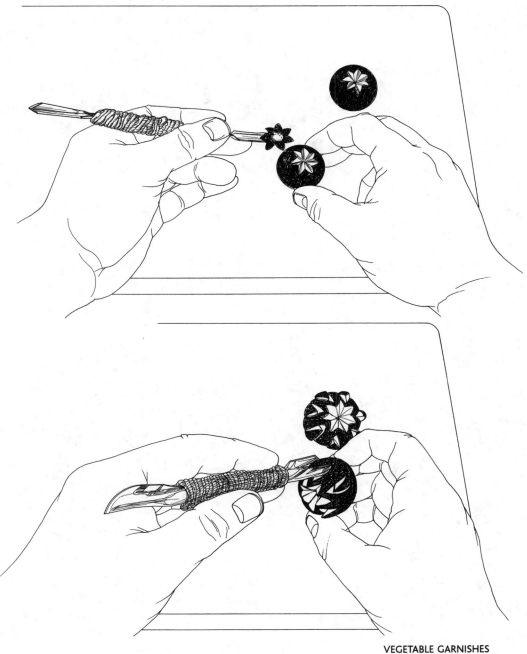

RADISH ROSETTE II

Make an incision down to approximately ¼ inch (6 mm) from the bottom of a radish, dividing it in two equal sections (still attached at the bottom). Make a second cut perpendicular to the first, dividing the radish into four quarters. Using a *V*-shaped cutter or bird's-beak knife, cut two wedges vertically into each quarter, leaving both still attached to the bottom of the radish. Place in ice water to allow the twelve wedges to open.

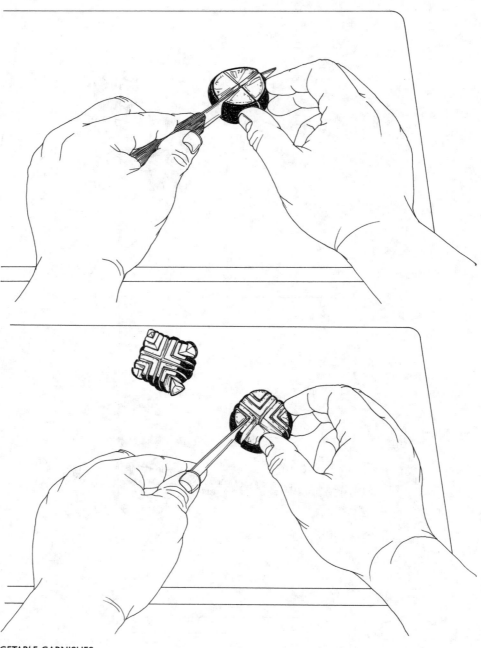

RADISH ROSETTE III

Make three incisions down to approximately ¼ inch (6 mm) from the bottom of a radish, dividing it in six equal wedges (still attached at the bottom). Using a *V*-shaped cutter or bird's-beak knife, cut a second vertical wedge into each of the six wedges, leaving each wedge still attached to the bottom of the radish. Place in ice water to allow the twelve wedges to open.

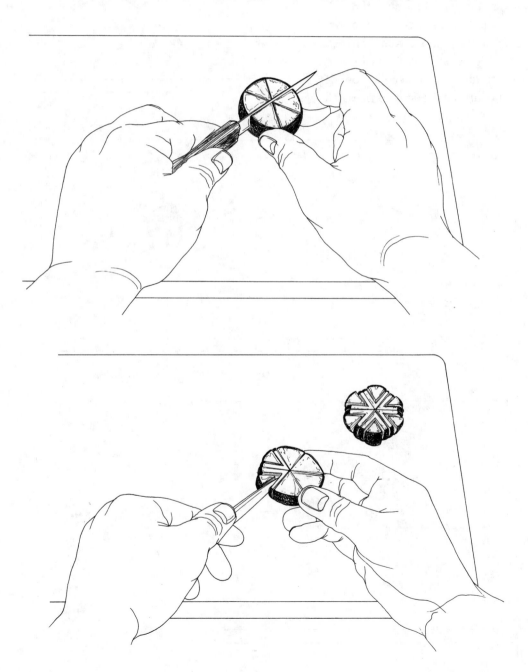

RADISH LANTERN

Lanterns are best made on radishes that are fairly large and elongated. Trim one end of the radish, then make four equally spaced, 45-degree, angled, flat cuts around the stem end. Recut behind each of these flat planes, not quite all the way through them, to create four petals. Repeat a row of flat cuts slightly above and between the petals of the first row. Recut behind each of these to create a second row of petals, then continue the same process all the way up the radish.

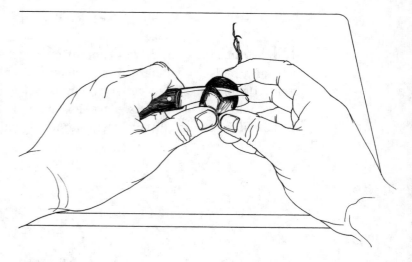

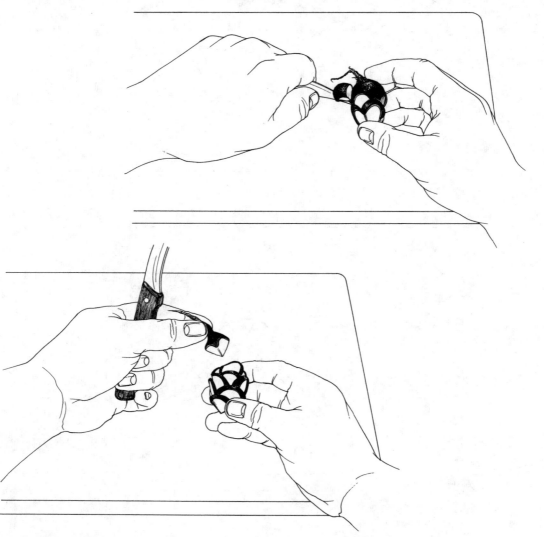

RADISH WHEEL

Picture light markings on the exterior of a radish that divide it into six or eight equal sections (depending on the size of the radish). Using a paring knife, make an incision on one of these imaginary lines, pointed toward the center, about ⅛ inch (3 mm) deep and running from one end of the radish to two-thirds of the way toward the other end. Make a second incision to one side of each of these incisions, cutting inward so that it intersects with the first incision, freeing a small wedge. Repeat this cut all the way around the radish. Invert the radish and make the same pair of incisions in the opposite direction.

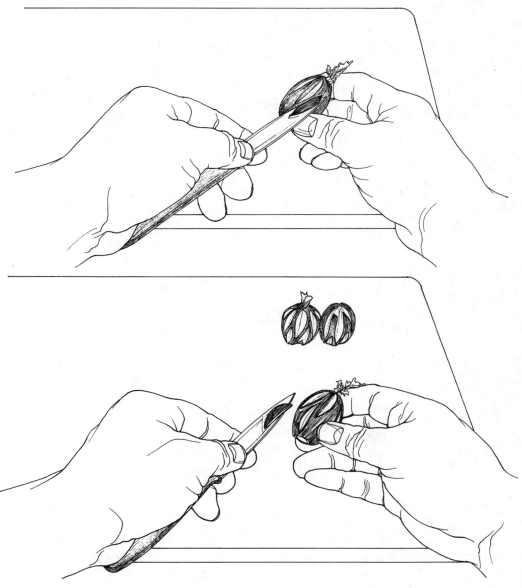

Tomato

TOMATO ROSE I

Select an unblemished tomato with a bright, red color. Begin by slicing a 3/4-inch (19-mm) round slice of skin from the bottom of the tomato, continuing that cut in a spiral fashion to remove a strip 1/2 inch (13 mm) wide. Continue cutting this thin, spiral strip around the tomato up to the top, where it will disconnect. Beginning where the strip ends, reroll it, skin-side outward, all the way back to the bottom round slice (which will act as a miniature base for the flower). Cover and refrigerate until ready to serve. *Note:* Be sure the strip is cut as thin as possible without breaking, so that it can be easily rolled up.

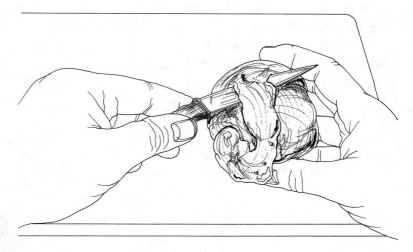

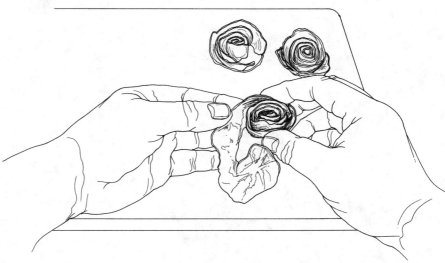

TIP *As visually stunning as this flower is, a rolled-up strip of tomato skin does not always fulfill the highest standards of gastronomic excellence. You may wish to consider the updated innovation that follows.*

TOMATO ROSE II

Cut a small-to-medium ripe tomato in half through the core. Place one of the halves cut-side down on a cutting surface and slice off one end—about ¼ inch (6 mm). Repeat a series of parallel cuts, extremely thin (the thinner the better), all the way through the tomato and across to the opposite end. Fan the tomato vertically in a long line, then roll the fanned-out tomato into itself.

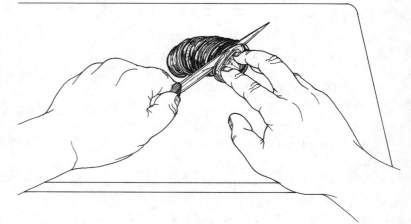

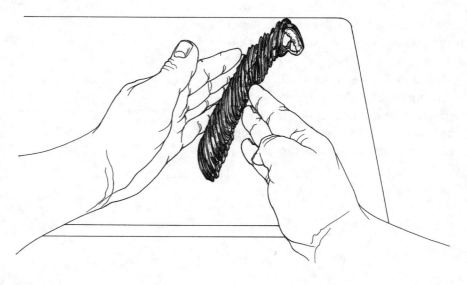

TOMATO WING

Cut a tomato in half and set the cut side down on a cutting surface. Cut a small wedge, 50 to 55 degrees wide, from the top center of the tomato; set it to one side. Repeat a series of wedge cuts down into the tomato to within approximately ¼ inch (6 mm) of the bottom. Reassemble all the wedges; set to one side. Lift the base up and carefully cut two thin slices from the sides (these will be the side wings). Set the base back down and reset the cut wedges in place. Slide the wedges out in one direction and curl the two thin side slices outward. Cover and refrigerate until ready to serve.

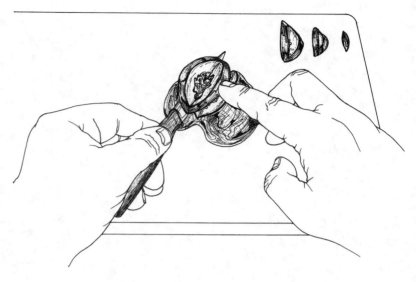

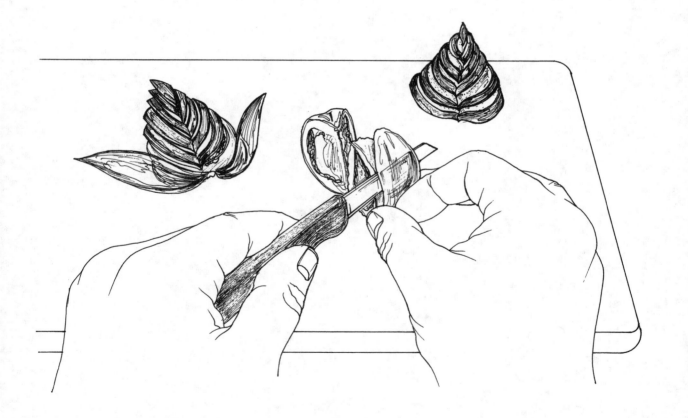

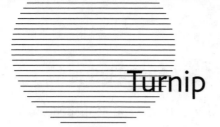

Turnip

TURNIP CALLA LILY

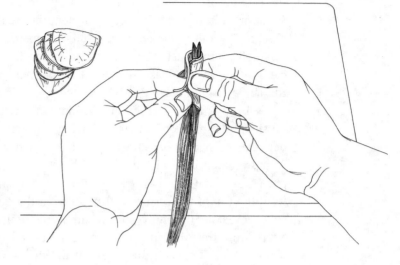

Blanch a dark green leek or scallion leaf in boiling, salted water for about a half minute or until limp enough to use as a tie (be careful not to overcook). Cool and set aside.

Cut several paper-thin slices of a small-to-medium, white turnip or daikon using a mandoline or electric slicer. Wrap a slice of turnip around one end of the scallion as firmly as possible, holding it in place with thumb and forefinger. The top of the slice of turnip should be close to the top of the scallion. Wrap a second slice around and slightly below the first slice. Wrap a third slice around the flower, flip one side back, and secure temporarily with a toothpick. Wrap securely with a strip of blanched green leaf, then remove toothpick. Cover and refrigerate until ready to use.

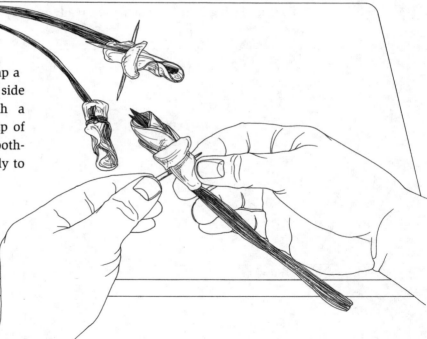

T I P *The purple tint on the top portion of the turnip can add an attractive, colorful element; peel the turnip if you prefer not to include it.*

TURNIP MARIGOLDS

This family of flowers is carved using the *U-* and *V*-shaped tools described in the section on Specialty Tools. Begin by removing a slice, approximately 2 inches (50 mm) round, from the top of a medium-to-large white or yellow turnip. Score a ½-inch (13-mm) circle in the center of this cut surface using a parisienne scoop or small, round pastry cutter. With a paring knife, shave the area around this circle, going down at least ⅛ inch (3 mm) at its base. Trim the outside top edge of the circle so that it is slightly rounded.

With a small *V*-shaped cutter, make a series of five to eight cuts around the outside of the scored circle, allowing a little space—about ⅛ inch (3 mm)— between each cut. Be sure to pop out and remove the little *V*-shaped pieces of turnip created by each cut. Recut directly beneath each of the shapes, leaving a petal ⅟₁₆ inch (1 mm) thick. Now cut a horizontal slice, ⅛ inch (3 mm) thick, from the top of the turnip, cutting in from the outside edge and stopping just outside the petals. Carefully remove the horizontal slice, leaving the *V*-shaped petals emanating from the outside edge of the center circle. Cut a second row of petals in the spaces between the petals of the first row, and remove a second horizontal slice as well. At this point, you may either cut a third row or simply remove the flower, placing it in ice water until ready to use.

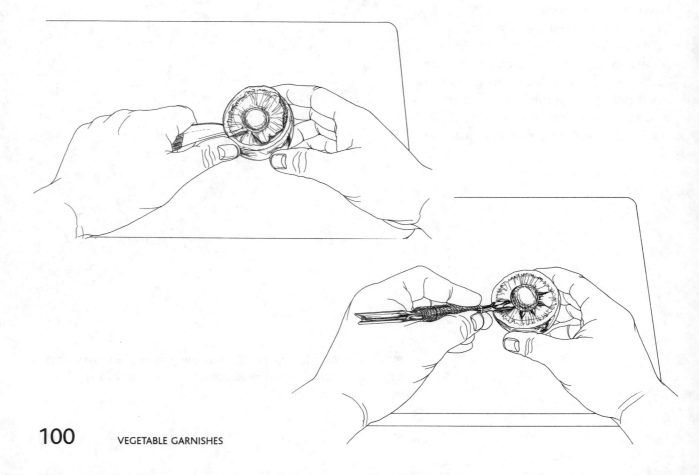

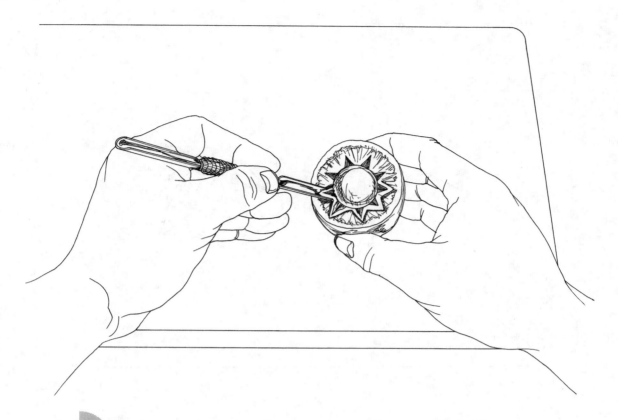

TIP *The U-shaped cutters can be used in exactly the same fashion to create a flower with rounded petals.*

Innumerable variations are possible using this technique—for example, following a row of U-shaped petals with a row of V-shaped petals (or vice versa). The size of the round center may be increased to 1 inch (26 mm) or more.

Try cutting the petals so that they are pointed off center.

These flowers can also be carved into daikon, yellow beet, and butternut squash. Though the latter has beautiful color, it tends to be fairly soft and does not hold up well.

You may prefer a more organized row pattern for this flower— an even number of petals followed by a second row of petals cut directly in between the row above it. More reckless muki-mono practitioners may throw caution to the wind and simply cover the surface of a turnip with as many petals as they wish, one right after the other, not necessarily in clean, organized rows. This is just another style approach.

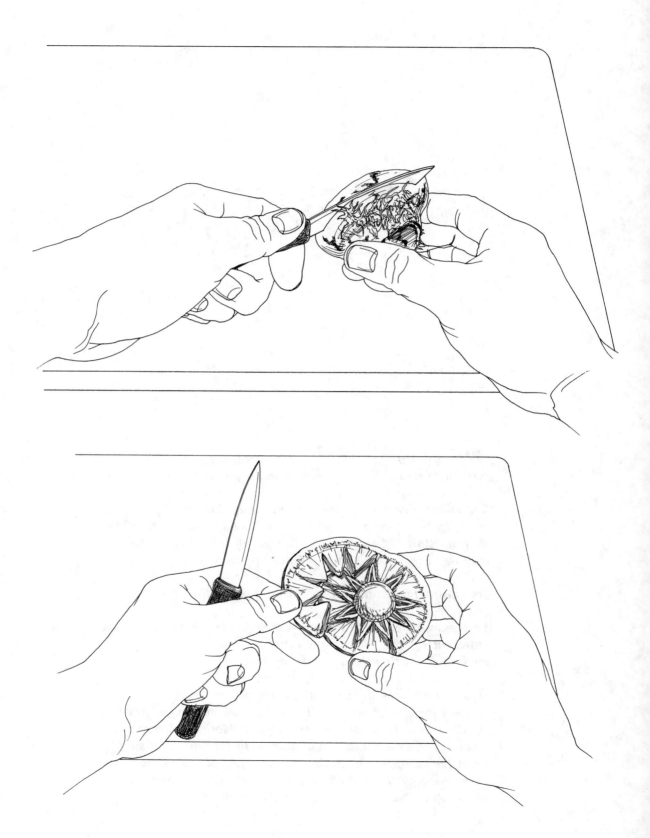

VEGETABLE GARNISHES

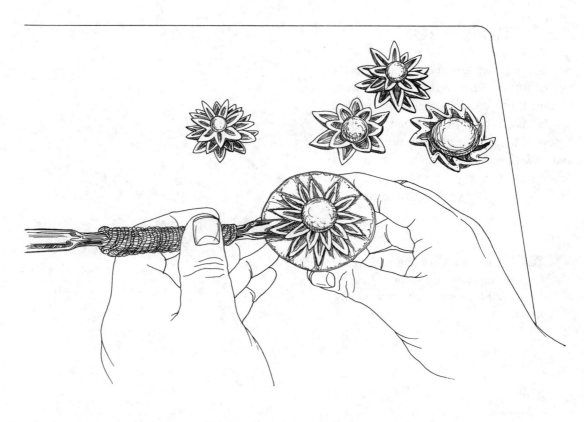

TURNIP ROSE

Cut five petals around the bottom of a peeled turnip. Shave a thin strip of turnip behind those cuts. Cut a second row of petals, each one in between the two below it, then shave another thin strip inside of that second row. Repeat this process all the way up the turnip, then place in ice water until ready to use.

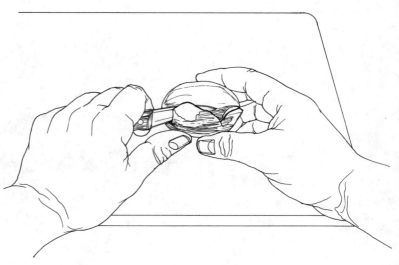

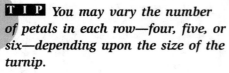 **TIP** *You may vary the number of petals in each row—four, five, or six—depending upon the size of the turnip.*

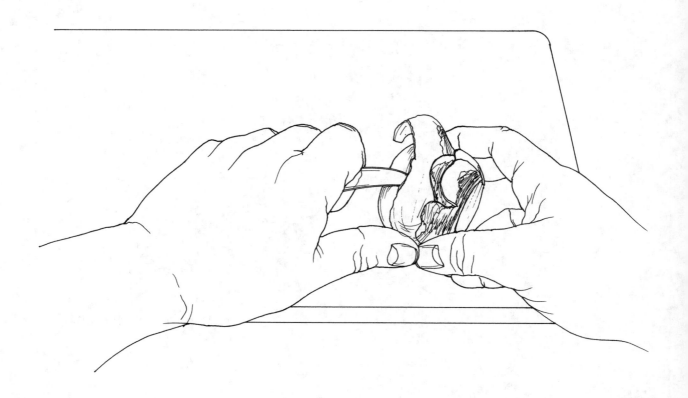

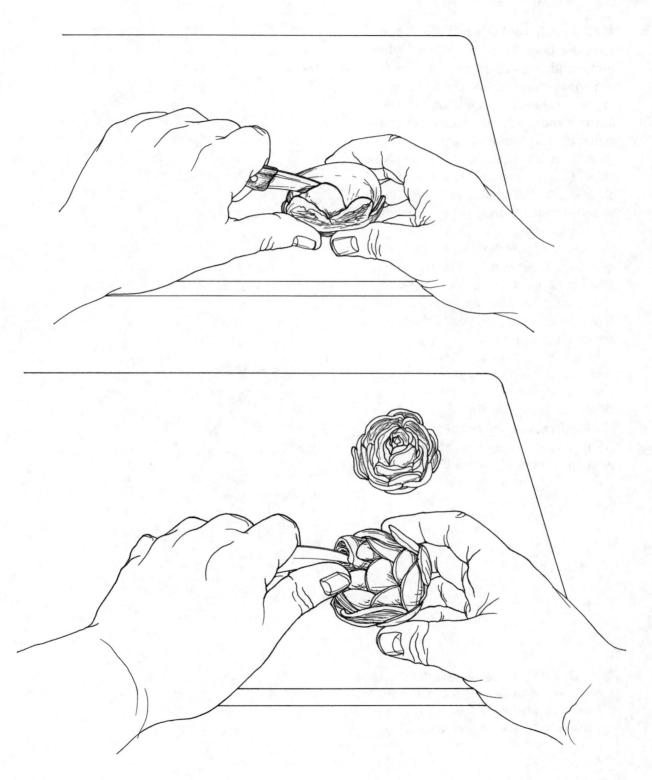

TURNIP SUNFLOWER

Peel a turnip and cut it into slices 1 inch (26 mm) thick. Score the center of the turnip with a small round pastry cutter or parisienne scoop; this circle can be ½ to 1 inch (13 to 26 mm) in diameter. With a paring knife, shave the area around this center circle, cutting down at least ¼ inch (6 mm) into the turnip at the base of the circle. Soften the outside top edge of the circle so that it is slightly rounded. Cut a series of radial grooves extending from the outside edge of the center circle to the outside edge of the turnip slice. These grooves will delineate the petals, so the space between them can vary considerably. Trim the outside bottom edge of the turnip slice so that the edge of the petals are thin and delicate.

Next, cut a small, rounded *V* at the point where the radial grooves intersect with the edge of the flower. Now cut an additional triangular groove at the base of each petal, running from the inner circle up to roughly the center of each petal. Place in ice water until ready to use.

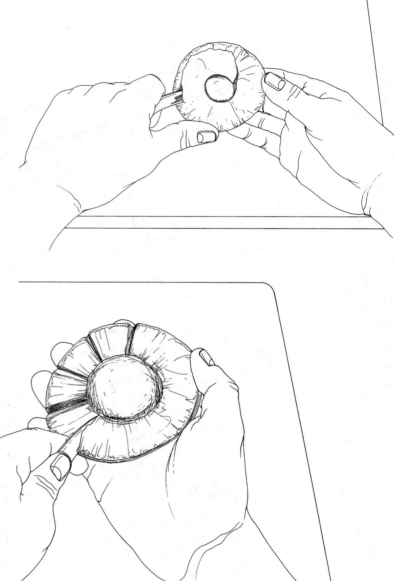

TIP *This flower can be blanched in boiling, salted water, brushed with butter, sprinkled with brown sugar, and baked until tender and glazed.*

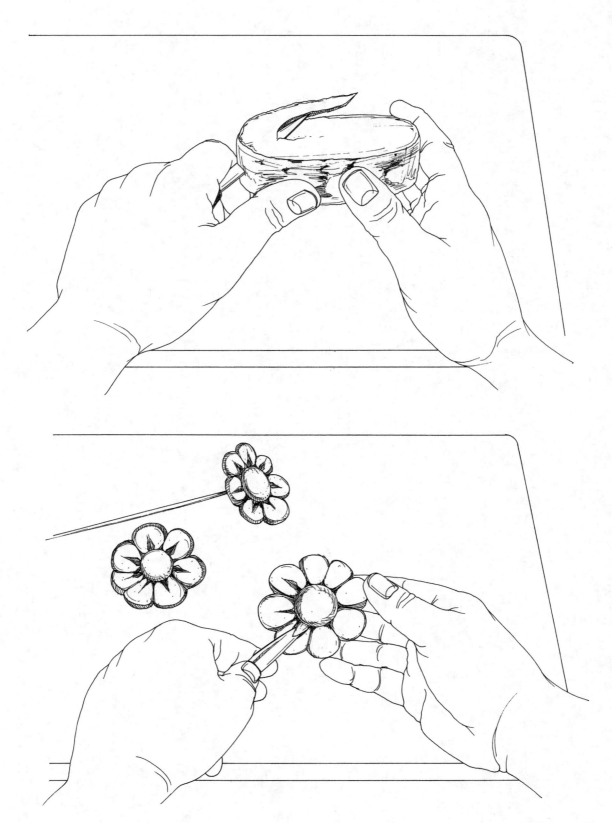

Zucchini

ZUCCHINI CROWN

With the knife positioned perpendicular to the zucchini, cut a zigzag around its circumference by inserting the knife into and slightly past the radial center. Make the first cut by sliding the knife into the zucchini, then pulling it down slightly. Make the second cut at a 45-degree angle from the top point of the first cut. Repeat these two cuts around the exterior until the end of the last cut meets the bottom of the first, then separate the zucchini into two parts. Variations in the length of the cuts and their angles allow an infinite number of variations in the finished flower form.

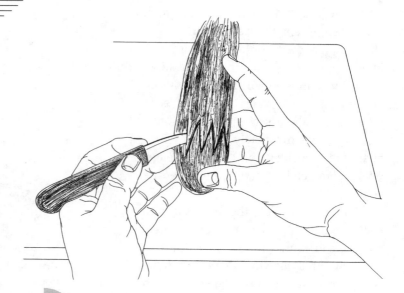

TIP *This basic cutting technique can also be applied to other fruits and vegetables, including cucumber, melon, onion, orange, radish, yellow squash, and tomato.*

ZUCCHINI ASTER

Remove the ends of a large zucchini, then slice it lengthwise on an electric slicer or mandoline into pieces approximately $\frac{1}{16}$ inch (1 mm) thick. The slices must be thin enough to roll without cracking. Set two slices on top of each other and make a series of parallel cuts widthwise, approximately $\frac{1}{8}$ inch (3 mm) apart and $\frac{3}{8}$ inch (10 mm) from one edge, while completely through the opposite edge.

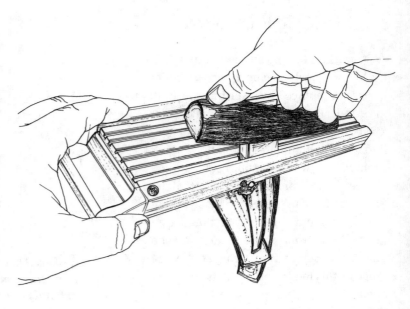

Carefully roll up the two zucchini slices, leaving a space of approximately $\frac{3}{8}$ inch (10 mm) in the center. Insert a medium pitted olive in the opening in the center, press it in gently, and secure with a toothpick. Place in ice water briefly until ready to use. *Note:* You may need to gently coax the petals outward when you are ready to present the flower.

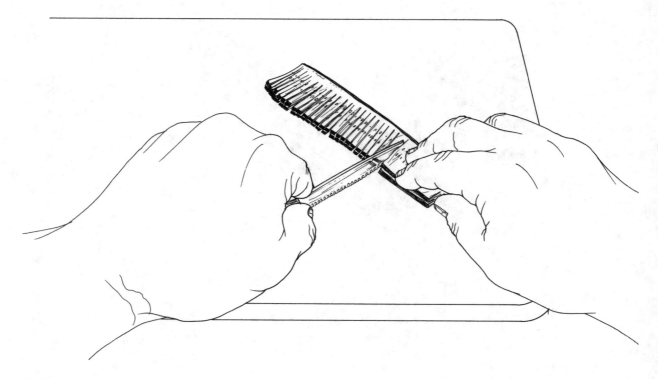

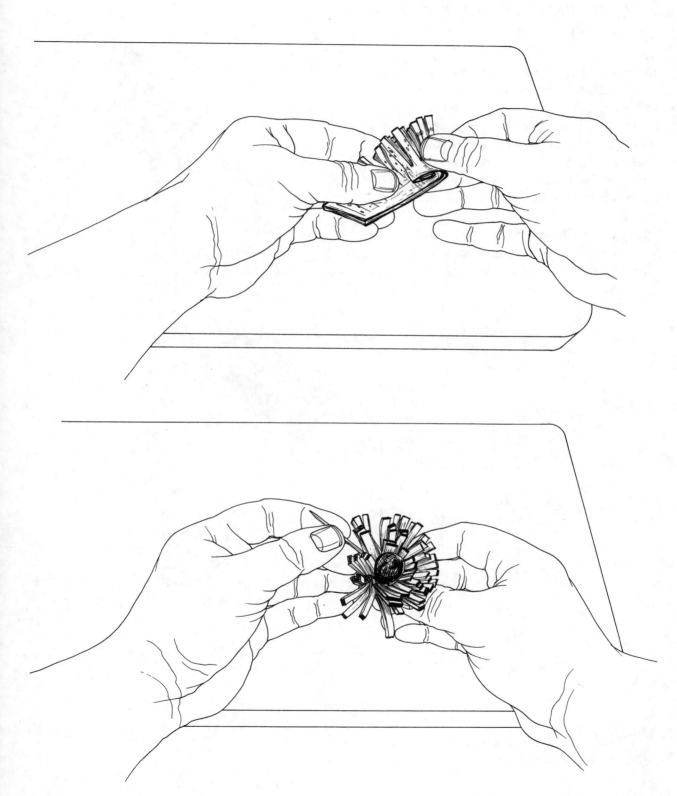

ZUCCHINI FIVE-PETAL FLOWER

Remove the bottom end (the stem end) of a zucchini. Make five incisions down into the zucchini at an angle of approximately 30 degrees. The top of each petal should be thin at the top and slightly thicker at its bottom. Gently twist the flower off and place in ice water to allow the petals to curl outward. *Note:* If you cut the petals just right, the point at which the petals intersect at their base will yield a small short strip that, when placed in ice water, will curl outward with the petals.

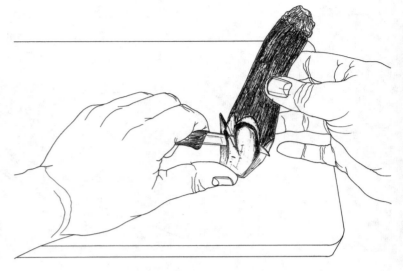

TIP *This flower can be also cut on yellow zucchini and cucumber.*

LATTICE SQUASH COLLAR

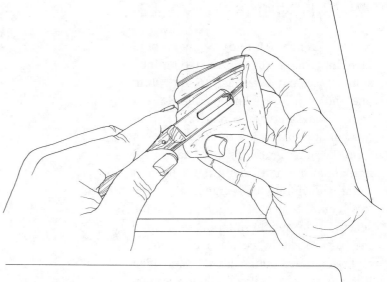

Cut a segment of a large, fat zucchini to 2 to 2½ inches (50 to 63 mm) long. Using a channel knife, cut a series of parallel grooves at about a 30-degree angle around the segment from one end to the other. Leave about ½ inch (13 mm) of space between each channel. Repeat the channel cuts across the first series of cuts in the opposite angle. Using a paring knife or a small, round pastry cutter, cut out the interior center of the segment, leaving the wall of the collar approximately ¼ inch (6 mm) thick. Place in ice water until ready to use. *Note:* The ends of the julienned vegetables extending out from the collar can be trimmed straight across or at an angle. Also, you may choose to cut only the first series of parallel cuts into the collar (see color photo of collars).

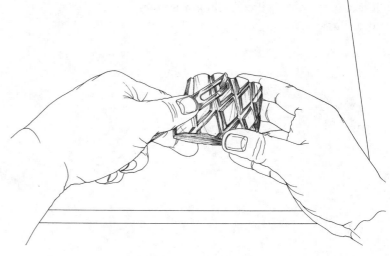

TIP *This collar is intended for use as a holding device for julienned vegetables—asparagus, bell pepper, carrot, celery, string beans, and so on. It should be blanched very briefly in boiling, salted water before use.*

This garnish can also be prepared with cucumber, butternut squash, yellow squash, and so on.

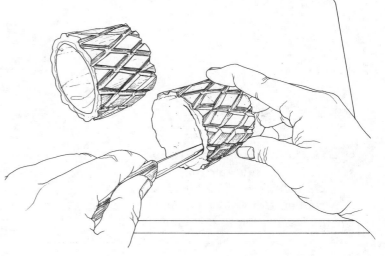

ZUCCHINI BARREL SOCLE

Cut a 2-inch (50-mm) segment of a medium-to-large zucchini. Make an incision approximately ¼ inch (6 mm) from one end of the segment, parallel to that end surface and down halfway. Repeat this cut approximately ¼ inch (6 mm) in from the other end. Make two additional horizontal incisions along the sides and slightly down into the segment to remove this center piece. Using a parisienne scoop, clean out the interior area. Store the barrel socle in ice water or wrapped and refrigerated until ready to use. Blanch it briefly in lightly salted boiling water before filling.

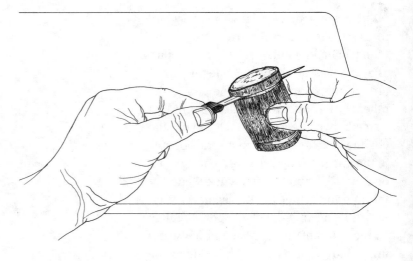

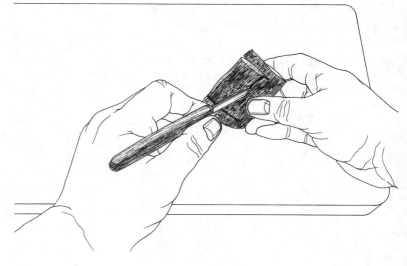

TIP *This socle can be used to serve a heated sauce or condiment, or a chilled sauce, salsa, or relish. A variation: Use yellow zucchini; cut the segment on a 45-degree bias.*

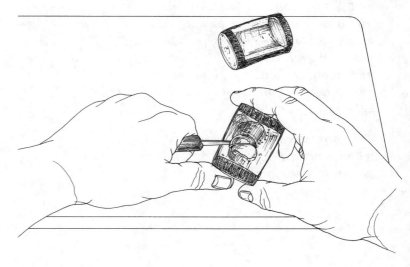

ZUCCHINI SPAGHETTI

Though not exactly a floral piece, this is an excellent way to cut and serve zucchini—as a hot vegetable (sautéed in olive oil, with garlic and mint chiffonade); as a salad (seasoned with a vinaigrette and included with an antipasto); as a delicate vegetable garnish in a broth-based soup. To cut the spaghetti, remove and discard the ends of a medium-to-large zucchini. Fit a Japanese mandoline with the medium julienne blade and place over a large bowl. Run the zucchini over the mandoline three or four times on one side. Turn the zucchini 90 degrees and repeat on that side. Repeat this process two additional times. Use the remaining center part of the zucchini in a puréed or creamed vegetable soup. Blanch the zucchini spaghetti in boiling, salted water for about one minute. Drain, cool, cover, and refrigerate until use.

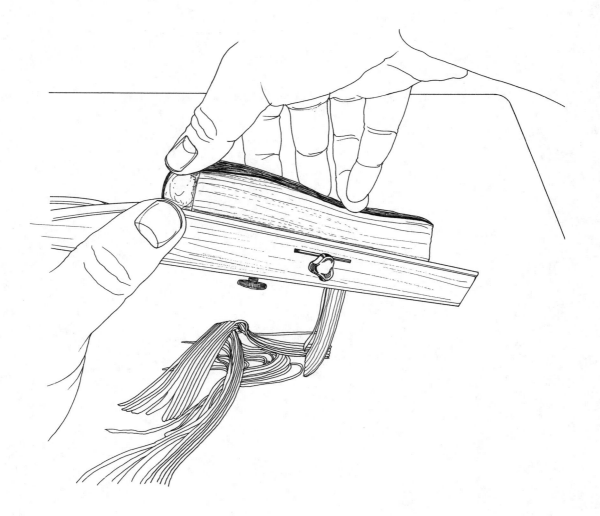

Fruit Garnishes

Fruit, in all of its many different flavors, colors, shapes, and varieties, represents hospitality and passion and warm reception. Thus, when fruit is carved for presentation, these essential characteristics are enhanced.

As with vegetables, a fruit garnish may indicate its presence within a dish. An excellent example is Diplomat Pudding, in which a variety of diced fruit blended with bavarian cream might be encased within a layer of lady fingers or sliced brioche. The same varieties of fruit contained within can be presented in a visually creative manner on the exterior.

There are also a number of primary dishes upon which fruit garnishes work well: orange starbursts, spiked wedges, or twisted slices on a platter of Roast Duckling Bigarade (a classical version of *à l'orange*); looped lemons, lemon starbursts, or twisted lemon slices with Lemon Chicken; an apple feather or apple fan with Roast Loin of Pork, Normandy Style.

And, finally, any solo presentation of fruit—a large platter on a buffet, for example—presents an opportunity for the creative use of all varieties of fruit as a garnish, sometimes in very uncomplicated ways. A few examples are the rococo apple technique applied to cantaloupe; a border of peach wedges with halved strawberries; a cascading row of sliced, peeled melon; and paper-thin slices of apple fanned out on opposing ends of a platter.

Apple

APPLE FAN

Cut an apple into quarters and trim the core by removing it with one straight, flat cut. Using a mandoline, cut the apple into very thin slices; dip them briefly into a lemon bath. Arrange six to twelve (or more) of these elongated half-circle slices on a plate, platter, or small wedge or block of cheese. Create the form of a fan by setting the slices down so that they emanate from the same point. These slices can also be used as a border on a fruit plate, or on a Brie cheese, or with any dish in which apples are an ingredient.

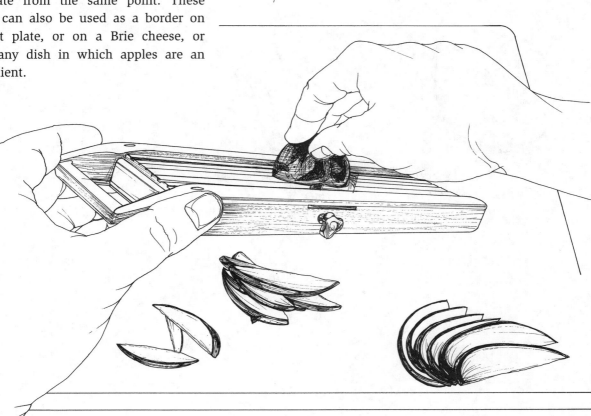

TIP *Consider how much tastier fruits and vegetables are when they are sliced paper-thin.*

APPLE FEATHER

Cut an apple lengthwise into quarters and trim the core of each quarter with a single, straight slice. Set an apple quarter on the work surface, cut side down. Cut a small wedge at 50 to 55 degrees from the top center of the apple; set it to one side. Repeat the cut directly under the first cut; set that piece aside as well. The thickness of the wedges should not exceed ⅛ inch. Continue cutting wedges down into the apple to within approximately ¼ inch (6 mm) of the bottom. Brush all cut surfaces with lemon juice and return the wedges in the order they were removed. Slide the wedges out in one direction and serve with an appropriate dish. *Note:* The apple should be used within an hour or so of cutting because it will begin to oxidize, resulting in turning brown.

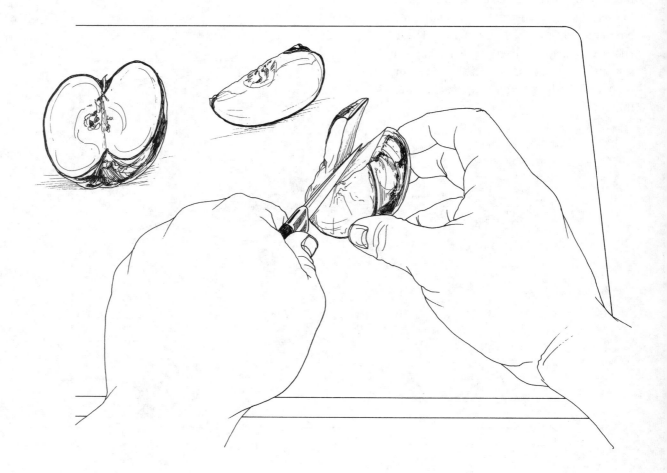

TIP *An apple feather is an excellent accompaniment to a cheese course, a fruit platter, or any dish with which a crisp, raw apple is harmonious.*

TIP *All of the forms and garnishes made with apple can also be created on any variety of pear.*

STEPPED APPLE FEATHER

Cut an apple into quarters lengthwise and trim the core of each quarter with a single, straight slice. Set an apple quarter on the work surface, cut side down. Cut a very small wedge at an angle of 50 to 55 degrees from the top center of the apple; set it to one side. Repeat the cut directly under the first cut; set that piece aside as well. The thickness of the wedges should not exceed ⅛ inch. Continue cutting wedges down into the apple to within approximately ¼ inch (6 mm) of the bottom. Brush all cut surfaces with lemon juice. Reassemble them, but separate from the base piece from which they were cut. Lay this reassembled wedge unit on the cutting surface and carefully cut it in half across its width. Reset these two halves into the base piece, sliding the severed wedges of each half outward and away from each other.

TIP *This stunning piece is quite beautiful all by itself, although it can also be used as a socle for chutney, relish, ground toasted nuts, or a mayonnaise-based sauce.*

ROCOCO APPLE

Create this small, extraordinary piece by cutting two apple feathers into the two upper quarters of a whole apple. Remove a thin slice of about ⅛ inch (3 mm) from the side of an apple and set it, cut plane down, on the cutting surface. Now imagine that the apple is divided into four equal quarters running lengthwise (horizontally, at this point); there are two quarters in the bottom half, and two in the upper half. Now simply cut two apple feathers into the two upper quarters, leaving a wall ¼ inch (6 mm) thick attached to the whole piece; separate the two feathers. After dipping all wedges in lemon juice, reassemble the two feathers in their respective quadrants, then slide the wedges out in opposite directions.

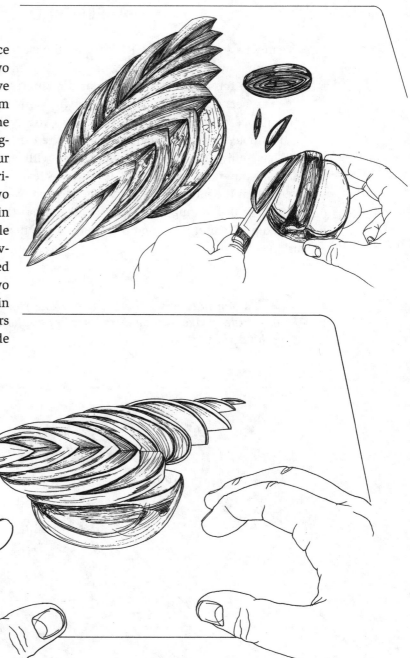

TIP *This technique also works exceptionally well with a melon such as canary, cantaloupe, or honeydew. Use as a centerpiece on a fruit platter.*

APPLE BIRD

Remove a ½-inch (12 mm) slice from the side of an apple. Set the apple cut-plane down onto the cutting surface. *Very important:* Save the slice. Visualize the top center of the apple as a quartered section and cut a feather into this section (six to eight wedges will suffice). Brush all surfaces with lemon juice and reset into the apple. Cut two smaller feathers into the sides of the apple, at a slight angle up toward the rear of the bird. These feathers will have only three to four wedges. Brush with lemon juice and set in place. Slide all three cut sections out toward the rear of the bird. At the front of the bird, at the intersection where the last top wedge was cut, make a small incision with a paring knife. Cut a wedge from the center of the initial cut slice, dip in lemon juice, and press one end of that wedge into that small incision.

TIP *You may wish to stick two whole cloves into each side of the top of the wedge, although the apple has the appearance of a bird without them.*

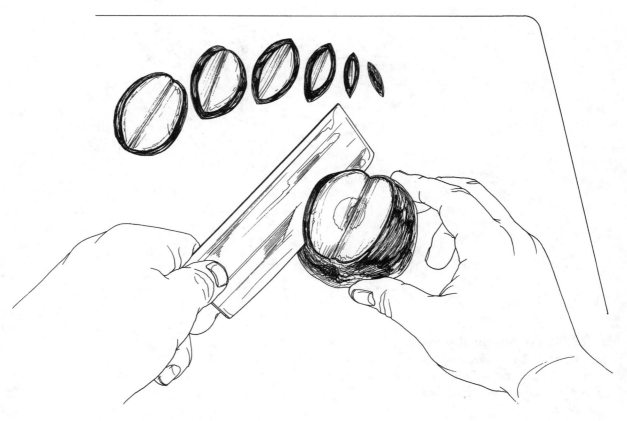

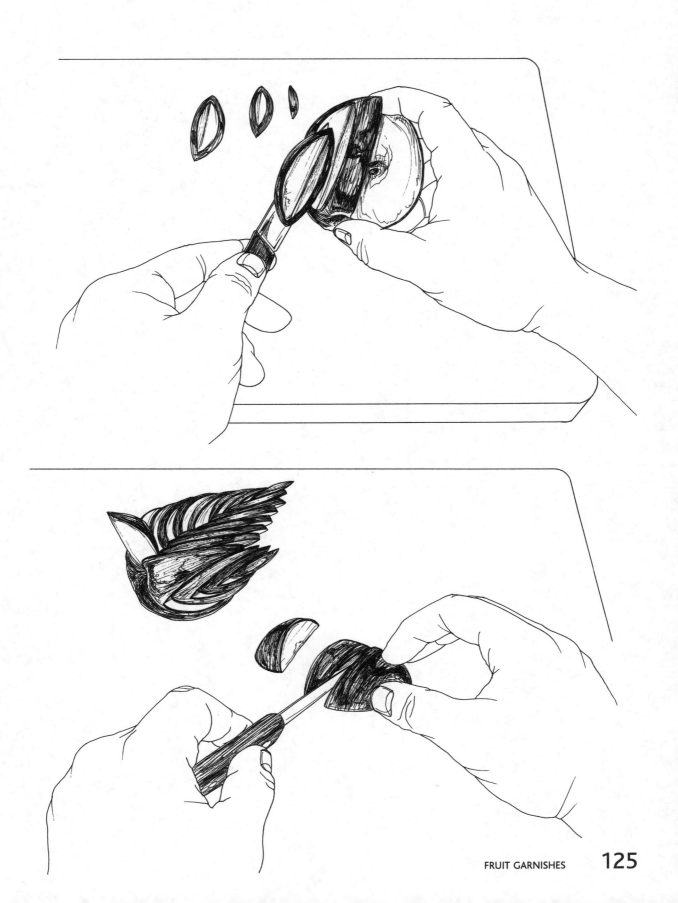

Lemon

LOOPED LEMON I

Remove a thin slice from each end of a lemon and cut the lemon in half. Using a channel knife, cut a strip of zest just under the center-cut edge, running about three-quarters of the way around the circumference. Carefully reverse the knife, pulling it off the strip and leaving the strip attached to the lemon. Repeat this technique just below the first strip, beginning on the side of the lemon opposite to where the first strip was cut, creating a second strip also running three-quarters of the way around the fruit. Now tie these two strips across the face of the cut surface in a square knot or some other interesting fashion. Use as a garnish for fish or with any dish where lemon in a welcome accompaniment. *Note:* The length of the strips can be increased, creating longer pieces with which to tie more complex knots.

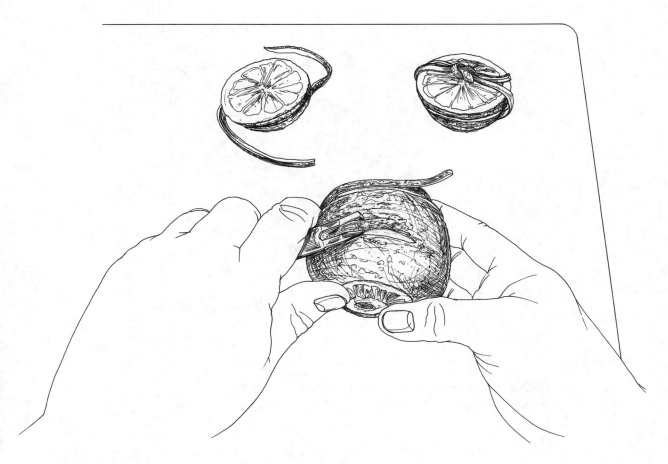

LOOPED LEMON II

Remove a thin slice from each end of a lemon. Using a channel knife, cut a strip of lemon zest beginning from the cut edge of one end down to a spot approximately ½ inch (13 mm) from the opposite edge. Do not separate the strip; instead, slide the channel knife back up and off the strip, leaving it attached to the lemon. Repeat this cut seven times, creating eight parallel strips equally spaced around the fruit. Turn the lemon over and repeat another eight cuts in the opposite direction and between the first eight strips.

Using a paring knife or bird's-beak knife, cut the lemon in half, pushing the lemon strips aside to avoid cutting them. Take the tip of a loop and turn it into itself at its base. Pressing it in gently, you may have to do this several times until it stays wedged in place. Repeat this with the other seven strips and the eight on the other lemon half. *Note:* If the lemon is old, the skin may be brittle, making this technique difficult. Use the previous technique instead.

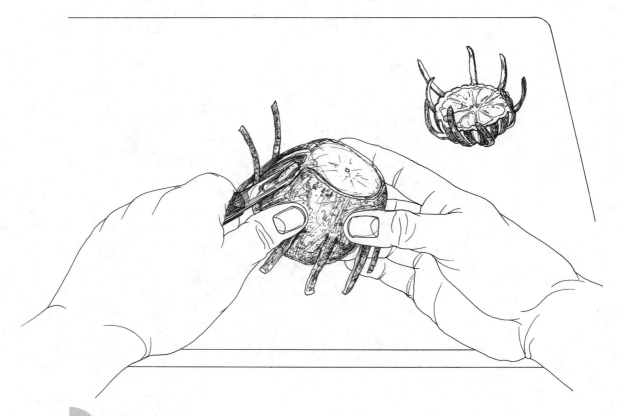

TIP *This technique can also be used on oranges and limes.*

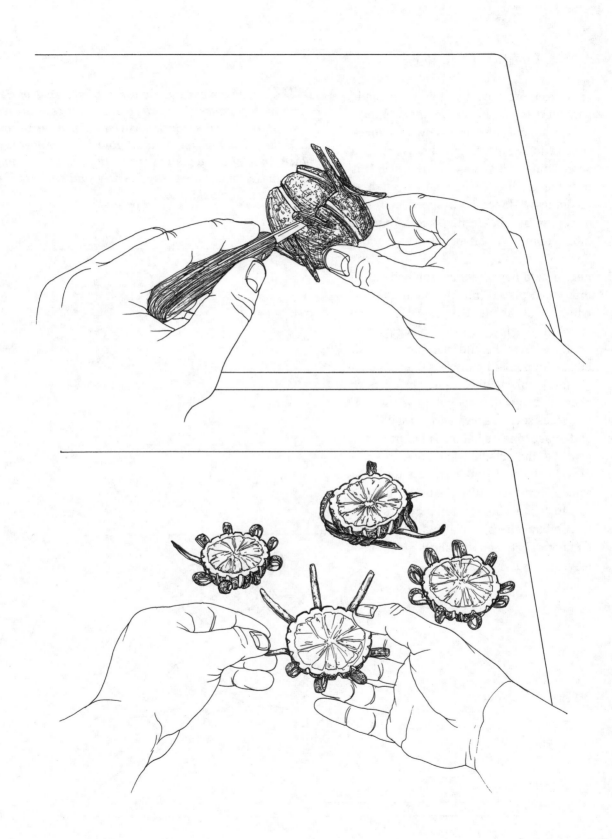

TWISTED SLICES

The secret to executing this very simple garnish is to cut the lemon, lime, orange, cucumber, zucchini, or yellow crookneck squash to the proper thickness. With a sharp knife and years of experience, it is possible to do this manually—but it is recommended, for both speed and efficiency, to use an electric slicer (found in most commercial kitchens) or a mandoline. When using an electric slicer, the item should have its ends trimmed flat so that when placed into the hand guard it will not roll about. *Warning:* Never use an electric slicer without placing your hand securely behind the hand guard. Slices should be slightly less than $1/16$ inch (1 mm) thick—thick enough to have some body, yet thin enough to be twisted.

Stack several slices on a cutting board and make one radial incision from the center to the outside edge. The slices can now be twisted and used on top of a salad, on a piece of grilled fish, or in a row to create a border. You may also wish to combine slices, such as a slice of cucumber in between two slices of lemon—or vice versa.

TIP *Hothouse cucumbers are the preferred variety to work with because they are cleaner and contain fewer seeds than the supermarket variety. For a variation, slice the cucumber on a mandoline at a 45-degree angle; place three slices together, make the radial incision lengthwise, twist them, then gently pull the slices apart to create unique shapes.*

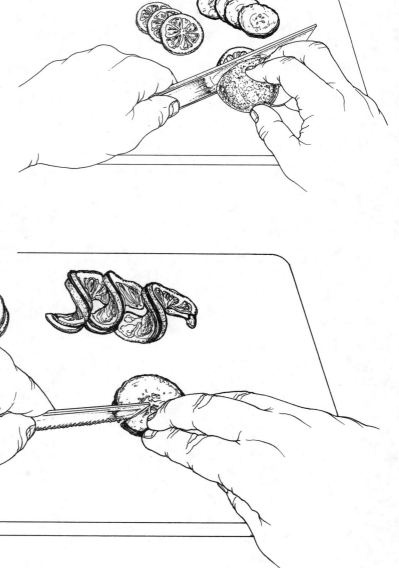

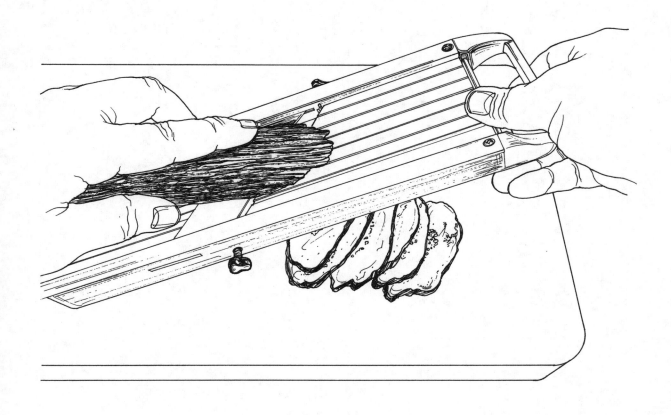

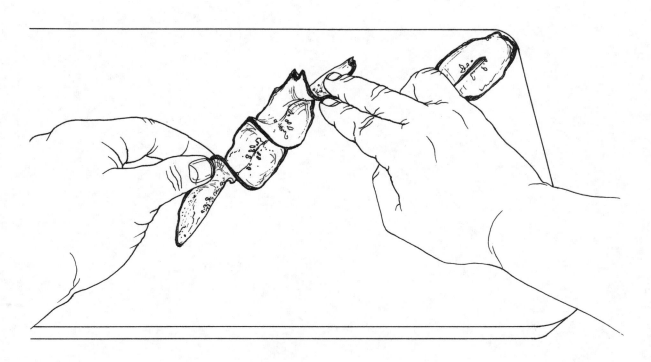

Melon

FIVE-PETAL CANTALOUPE BOWL

Lightly mark five equidistant points around the bottom of a cantaloupe. Make an incision from each mark in an *S* shape across to the other end of the cantaloupe. Repeat this cut nine times, separate the two halves of the melon, then scoop out and discard the seeds.

In each of the five petals on each half, make two additional incisions inside the petal, following its contour.

TIP *This melon functions very well as a bowl for cut melon or fruit salad.*

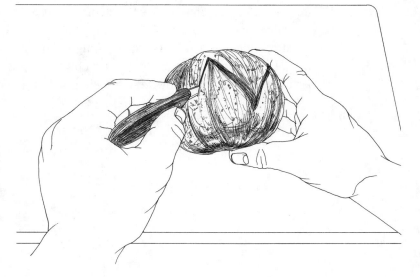

MELON LEAF

Remove a thin slice from a cantaloupe or honeydew melon. Remove a second, thick slice, cutting about one-quarter of the way across the melon (you should be able to just avoid the seeds). Place this slice cut-side down onto a cutting surface and cut in half diagonally. Trim each of the pieces in the shape of a curved teardrop.

Now make two parallel, slightly curved grooves down the center of each teardrop, leaving a raised strip running down the center of the leaf. Make a series of small grooves extending at an upward angle from both sides of the central grooves. Repeat this with the remaining melon as needed.

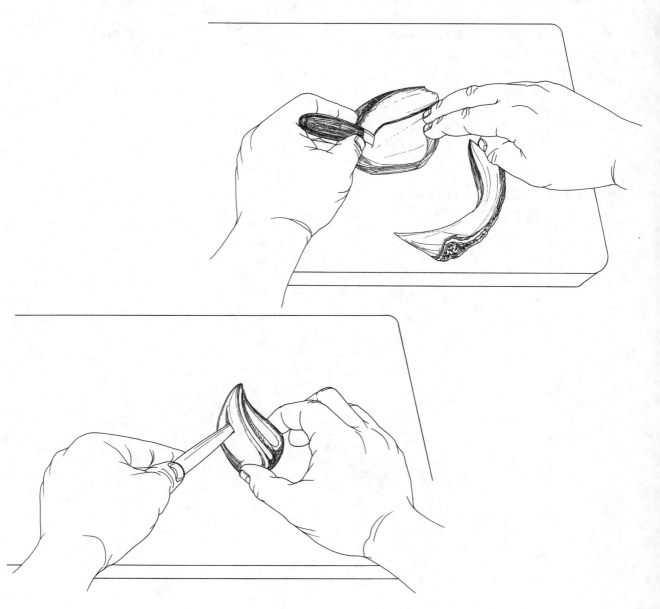

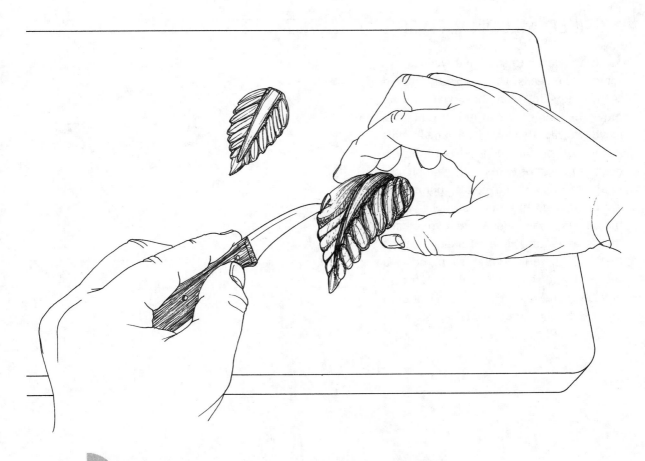

TIP *Other melons, such as canary, casaba, and watermelon, as well as apples, can be carved into these leaf forms.*

SPIKED MELON WEDGE

Cut a melon into six equal wedges and remove the seeds. Cut a slightly curved *V* into the skin, then slice away and remove the pointed half of the *V*. This will leave two slightly curved *V*-shaped petals in the skin of the wedge. Using a bird's-beak knife, carve two small, oval shapes in the middle of the petals, pointed at each end. Lightly score a straight *V* into the melon flesh above the two petals, then shave a thin sheet of melon outside that *V*. If there is enough room, score a second *V* and shave a thin sheet of melon outside that *V* as well. Trim the bottom of one end of the wedge to stand it upright.

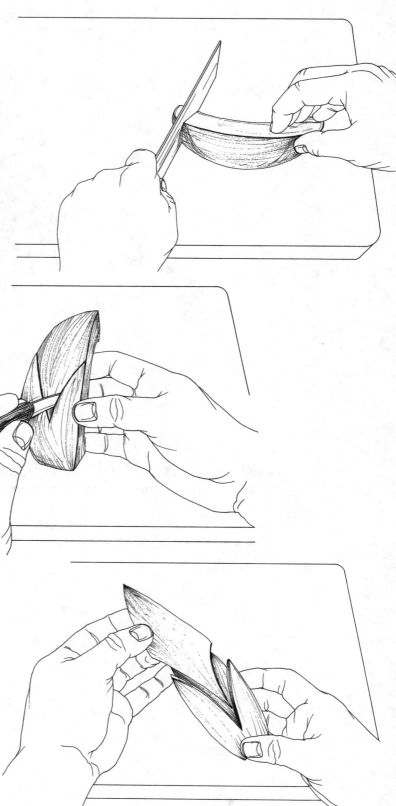

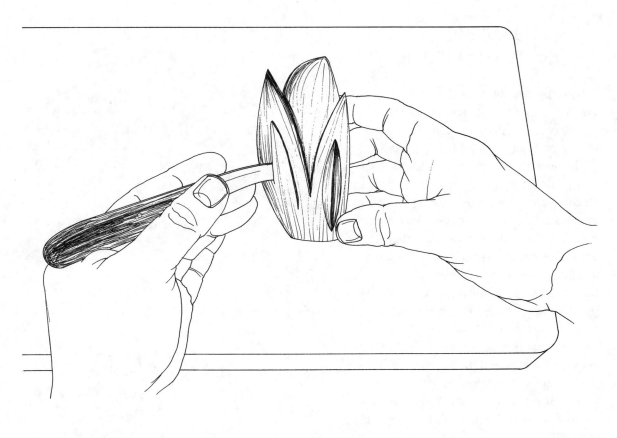

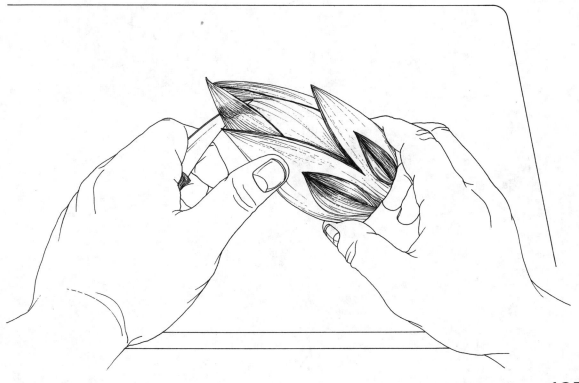

FLORAL MOTIFS
ON WATERMELON

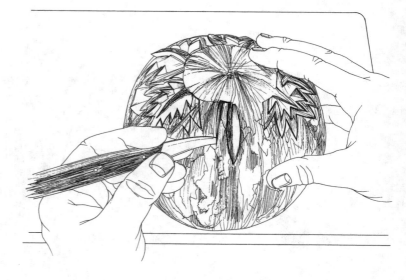

Begin by creating a leaf pattern on the green exterior skin of the watermelon.

Carve the patterns like the melon leaves (see page 132–133). Because the flesh beneath the green exterior is pale, you can obtain some gorgeous patterns. Once these are carved, the remaining melon surface can be shaved, leaving the pale, off-white flesh beneath. When this surface is cut into—about ¼ inch below its surface—the red flesh of the watermelon is revealed, allowing extraordinary possibilities for the mukimono artist. A motif of diamond (lozenge) shapes is common, as is a large rose, made with a series of curvalinear lines. Score a horizontal line about 3 inches from the bottom of the melon, to mark the external green skin from the pale white melon underneath.

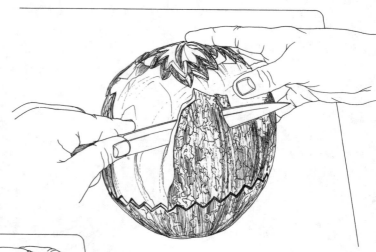

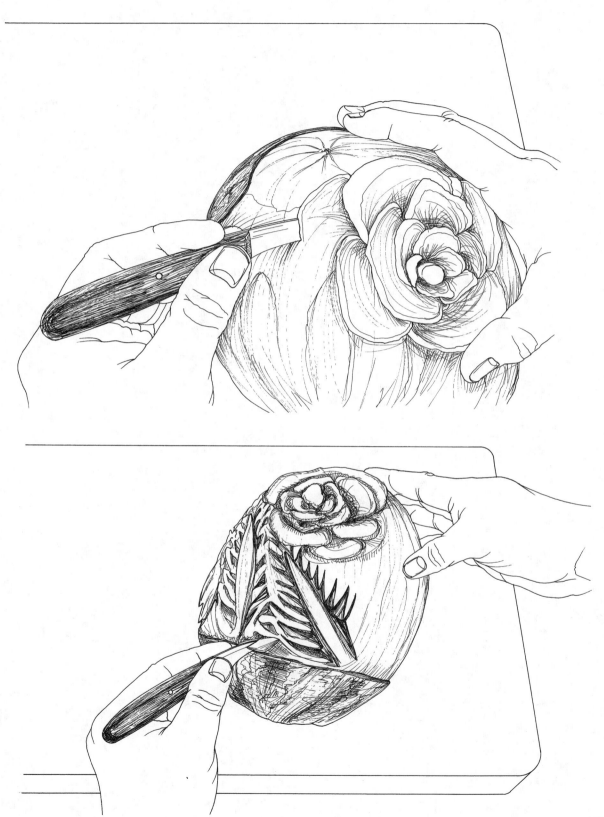

Orange

ORANGE STARBURST

Cut circles 1½ to 2 inches (38 to 50 mm) round from the exterior of an unblemished orange. Place cut side down onto a cutting surface. Cut a series of *V*s, about ¼ inch (6 mm) deep, around the outside of each circle, creating a series of points emanating from the center of the circle. Use as ornaments between the leaves of the Pineapple Christmas Tree (page 148–149) or stack them in pairs, holding them together with a half toothpick. Press a small grape, carrot ball, or small circle of orange skin to cover the portion of toothpick sticking out of the star.

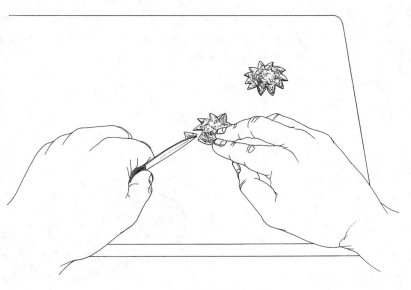

SPIKED ORANGE WEDGE

Remove a thin slice from the bottom of an orange, then cut the orange into eight equal wedges. Retrim the bottom so that each slice will stand on its own. Now make a *V* cut into the separated peel, approximately ¼ inch (6 mm) from the outside edge. Carefully trim a sheet of outside skin from the pith, beginning at the top, cutting not quite all the way down to the bottom. (The skin should still be connected at the bottom.) Trim the excess pith from the orange. When ready to serve, carefully turn the outermost piece of orange skin down into the wedge formed at the base of the orange.

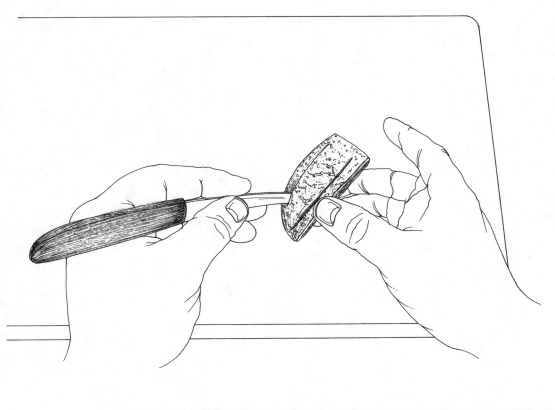

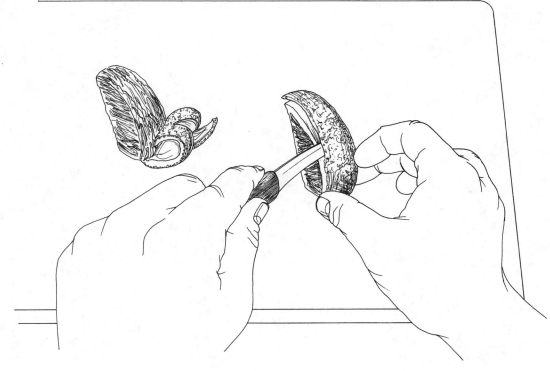

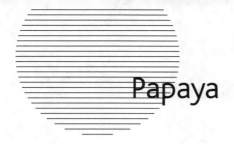

Papaya

GROOVED PAPAYA

Cut a papaya in half lengthwise, then scoop out and discard the seeds and connective material. Carefully peel the fruit; remove a slice from the bottom so that the half will stand upright. Lightly score a slightly curved *S* form in the papaya, running from the center of the fruit down to the two bottom outside corners. The score should be about ⅛ inch (3 mm) deep, so that when you shave the papaya just outside that score, a thin strip is removed. Repeat the score about ½ inch (12 mm) outside of the first score and remove another strip. Continue until the surface is covered with a series of stepped edges. *Note:* One variation to the *S* curve is an inverted *V*.

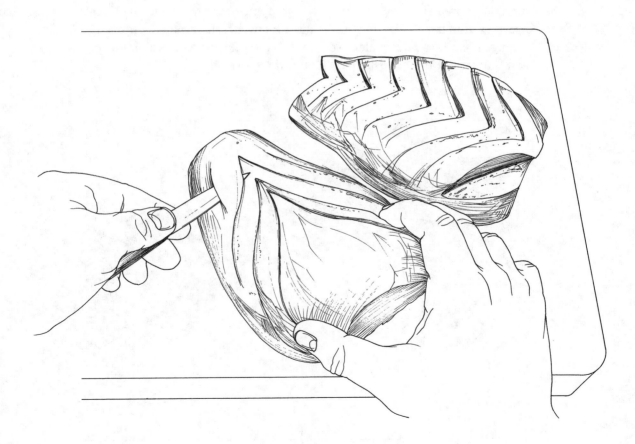

Pineapple

PINEAPPLE BOAT

Wash a ripe pineapple well in warm water; drain. Using a pair of scissors, snip the rough, damaged, or broken ends of the crown leaves. Cut the pineapple body in half, cutting the leaf crown in half at the same time (leave it attached). Place the cut side of the two halves down on the cutting surface and cut each in half, including the crown (still attached). Turn one of the quarters up onto its outside edge and, using a paring knife, make a horizontal incision about ½ inch (13 mm) below the top edge, just underneath the woody center. Continue cutting down around the flesh, freeing a large wedge of the pineapple flesh. (Because it is fairly wide, you may have to cut in from both sides of the bottom of the quarter.) Make a series of vertical incisions down into the loosened wedge approximately ½ inch (12 mm) apart, cutting the wedge into slices. Push the wedges alternately outward or arrange them in a wave pattern so that the slices extend outward on one end and outward in the opposite direction at the other end.

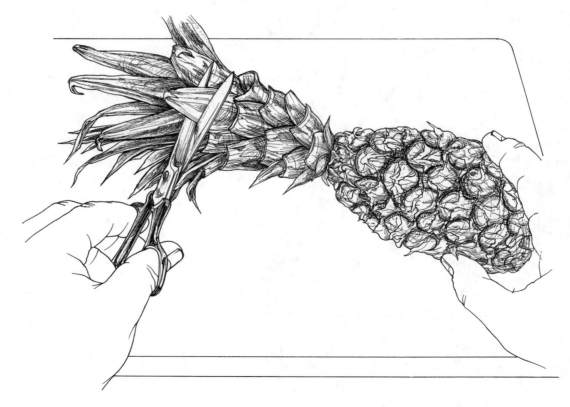

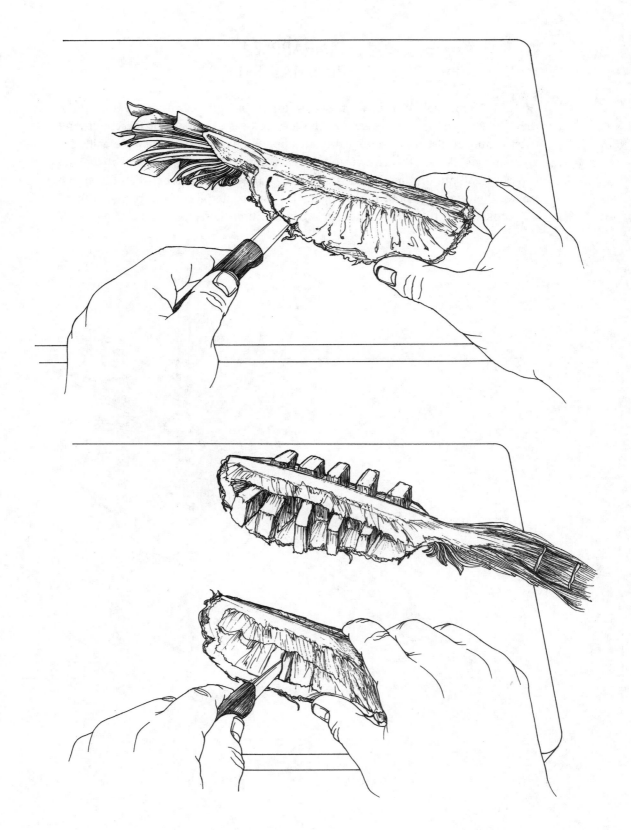

PINEAPPLE
CHRISTMAS TREE

Wash a pineapple well in warm water; drain. Using a pair of scissors, snip the rough, damaged, or broken ends of the leaves. Grasp the base of the crown and twist it until it disconnects from the pineapple body. (Set the pineapple aside for another use.) Invert the crown and press it down onto a plate so that the top leaves spread out on the plate. Insert a few Orange Sunbursts between the crown leaves, then dust with powdered sugar. Use as a centerpiece for a platter of holiday cookies, cut fruit, chocolates, or a combination thereof.

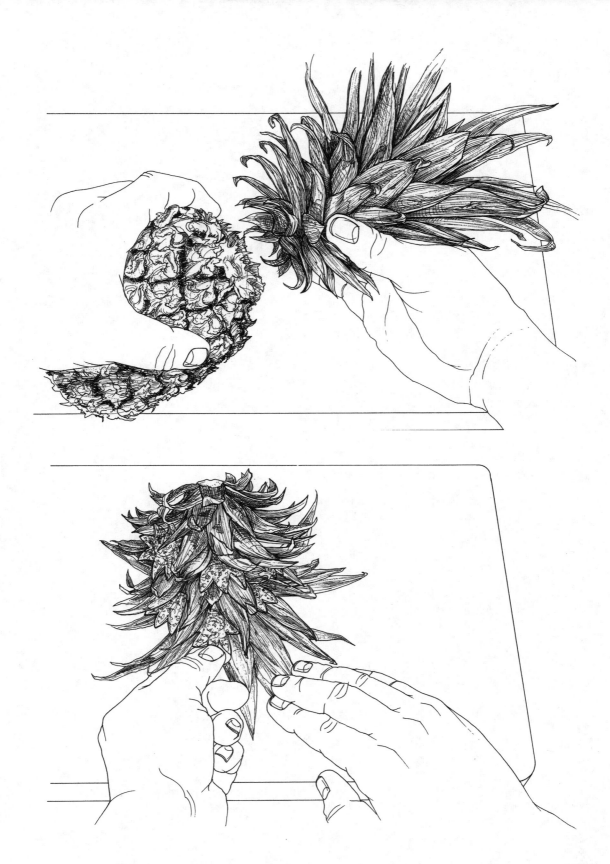

Appendix of Specialty Suppliers

Tools

J.B. Prince, 36 East 31st Street, New York, NY 10016; (212) 683-3553; (800) 473-0577; Fax: (212) 683-4488; Website: www.jbprince.com. Mail-order supplier of clothing, smallwares, and tools. Request current catalog.

Pro Chef International, 12656 Mengibar Avenue, San Diego, CA 92129; Phone: (858) 484-6423; Fax: (858) 484-0504. Specialty supplier of mukimono carving tools, high-quality ice-carving chisels and saws, and books on both subjects. Request current catalog.

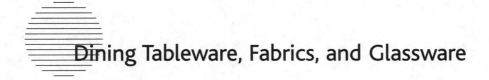

Dining Tableware, Fabrics, and Glassware

Robert King Associates, 166 Geary Street, Suite 1202, San Francisco, CA 94108; (415) 989-5866; Fax: (415) 989-5867; email: rbtking@worldnet.att.net. Distributors of several lines of exquisite plateware, table fabrics, and dining accessories from some of the finest manufacturers in the world.

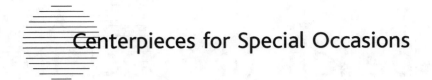

Centerpieces for Special Occasions

Culinart, Inc., 1948 West Eighth Street, Cincinnati, OH 45204; (513) 244-2999; (800) 333-5678; Fax: (513) 244-2555; Website: www.culinart.net. Suppliers of extraordinary tallow and chocolate sculptures and sculpting supplies, including a modern tallow sculpting medium. Mr. Dominic Palazzolo, president; Anita Wheeldon, contact person.

Cutlery

Russell Harrington Cutlery, Inc., 44 Green River Street, Southbridge, MA 01550; Phone: (508) 765-0201; Fax: (508) 764-2897; Website: www.russel-harrington.com; E-mail: sales@rhcutlery.com. Manufacturer of the Three-way Knife Sharpener.

Index